D1450410

WHEN IN
PARIS

The Ultimate Study-Abroad Guide

☑ Y0-CAW-541

Writer: Sara Heft
**SparkNotes would like to thank Margo Orlando for her editorial
contributions to this book.**

See page 237 for a list of photo credits.

Spark Publishing
A Division of Barnes & Noble
120 Fifth Avenue
New York, NY 10011
www.sparknotes.com

Library of Congress Cataloging-in-Publication Data

When in Paris: live like a local.
    p. cm.—(When In—)

 ISBN-13: 978-1-4114-9845-7 (pbk.)
 ISBN-10: 1-4114-9845-3 (pbk.)

 1. Paris (France)—Description and travel. 2. Paris (France)—Guidebooks. I. Spark
Publishing.

DC707.W58 2007
914.4'3610484—dc22

2007029508

Please submit changes or report errors to www.sparknotes.com/errors.

Printed and bound in the United States

10   9   8   7   6   5   4   3   2   1

A NOTE FROM SPARKNOTES

Congratulations on your decision to study abroad! Living in a new country, whether for a semester, a year, or longer, will enlighten you in ways you can't even imagine. Today, many consider travel abroad to be an essential step in a young person's education. Immersing yourself in a new culture, among new people, places, and things, will not only broaden your worldview, but also better equip you to face the challenges of a rapidly globalizing future.

We created the *When In* series to help you make the most of your time abroad. This book is intended for those who have already been accepted into a study-abroad program or have made the decision to live overseas. Your college or university will advise you about choosing a program, prerequisites and academic requirements, paperwork, and financial arrangements, so our focus is on the next step: the challenges you'll face as you settle into your new life. Our goal is to give you *exactly* what you need to know to make a smooth transition and get the most out of your time abroad.

Unlike traditional travel guides, the *When In* series focuses on the basics of living daily life as a study-abroad student:

- Nuts-and-bolts information, from finding housing to setting up a bank account to getting medical care

- The inside scoop on living on a student's budget

- The city's coolest restaurants, bars, clubs, study spots, and other places to hang out with friends

- Concise information on art, theater, film, music, sporting events, and other activities to keep you busy and involved in city life

With your *When In* guide, you'll *live like a local* in no time. Good luck!

Got comments? Your feedback makes us better. Contact us at www.sparknotes.com/comments.

KEY TO SYMBOLS

We use the following symbols throughout this guide:

Ⓐ	Address
Ⓣ	Telephone number
Ⓦ	Website
Ⓜ	Métro stop

10 TIPS FOR MAKING THE MOST OF YOUR TIME ABROAD

1. *Do* make friends with the locals. This will be one of the most rewarding aspects of your stay. Now's not the time to hold back!

2. *Do* take seriously every opportunity to practice speaking a new language. Immersing yourself in the language day in and day out will speed your learning process.

3. *Don't* worry about what you're missing back home. Do your best to live in the moment and embrace this amazing opportunity.

4. *Do* take advantage of cheap flights and train fares. You'll likely have frequent breaks—or, at least, greater freedom than you're used to—and it's easy and affordable to take weekend or even weeklong trips to new places.

5. *Do* keep a journal, create a blog, snap pictures, shoot videos, or otherwise record your time abroad. You'll want to remember and share all the details.

6. *Don't* be afraid to speak up if you find yourself facing anti-Americanism or stereotypes. Remember that you can counter negative stereotypes by setting a good example abroad.

7. *Don't* let culture shock get you down. Confusion is a normal part of travel, and only by taking time to settle in and make friends will you conquer it.

8. *Do* immerse yourself in the local culture. Eat what the locals eat. Shop where they shop. If you can't find a familiar item from home, live without it.

9. *Don't* embark on your experience with assumptions or preconceptions. Your new life will surprise you in every possible way—and you should let it.

10. *Don't* view your study-abroad time as your one and only chance to experience life abroad. Relish the everyday moments and reassure yourself that you'll be back!

Other titles in the **When In** series include:

CONTENTS

INTRODUCTION

Croissants, men in berets, skinny baguettes. Tiny dogs and cutting-edge fashion. The Champs Élysées, the Eiffel Tower, and the pyramid-shaped entrance to the Louvre. Cigarettes and long philosophical discussions at sidewalk cafés. Exquisite food and endless red wine. Your ideas of Paris probably encompass these images and more—of all the cities in the world, few capture the imagination as intensely as Paris.

The truth is that Paris is home to millions of people whose concerns about life, school, and work will probably seem pretty familiar. Even in this most postcard-perfect of cities, daily life has its own irritations and frustrations, and—contrary to what you may believe—plenty in Paris is less than beautiful. That said, Paris is utterly unique, and some of the images in your mind, like the amazing bakeries and the breathtaking art, will live up to every expectation. Parisians, and the French in general, have profound esteem for their history, culture, and traditions, and you'll begin to understand their passion as you settle into Parisian life.

HISTORY

One of the best parts about living in Paris is that there's history—literally—around every corner. From a twelfth-century fountain to the remnants of a medieval city wall, you can go back in time just by walking to the grocery store.

L'Île de la Cité, the island on the Seine that comprises the city's earliest center, was settled around 250 B.C.E. by the Parisii, a Celtic tribe that was eventually conquered by the Romans. After centuries of Roman rule, Paris was conquered by the Franks in the late fifth century and declared capital of Gaul under king Clovis in 508 C.E. The city saw much conflict in the centuries that followed, including raids by the Vikings, the Hundred Years' War, plague, English occupation in the fifteenth century, the Wars of Religion in the sixteenth century, and the French Revolution. This city also saw a parade of influential figures who took it upon themselves to shape—and rule—the city, including Louis XIV, the "Sun King" who built Versailles; Louis XVI, who incited his subjects to revolution in 1789; Marie-Antoinette, his queen, who became notorious for her spending habits and apathy toward her subjects; and Napoléon, who ruled the First Republic until his defeat and exile.

World Wars I and II were hard on France. The country emerged victorious from World War I, but it lost more than a million troops, and World War II left France deeply traumatized in the wake of years of Nazi occupation. Through it all, however, writers and artists were drawn to Paris, which is still a center of intellectual and creative innovation today.

Traces of what may seem like ancient history are still prominently on display throughout the city. For example, Napoléon III, who came to power in the mid-nineteenth century, brought about extensive architectural renewal led by urban planner Baron Haussmann. Napoléon III's goal was to eliminate narrow streets, where revolution fermented, and replace them with wide boulevards, parks, a modern sewer system, and stately façades. Today you can see Haussmann's legacy all over Paris in the wide, grand avenues and uniform (and lovely) wrought-iron balconies. History is everywhere in this most European of cities.

CULTURE

Paris is one of the largest cities in Europe, but you're unlikely to feel overwhelmed by the scale of things. In fact, the physical characteristics of the city are human size—there are virtually no skyscrapers, parks and gardens are everywhere, and the pace of life is far from frenetic once you're outside certain parts of the city center.

Parisians maintain an enviable quality of life, placing fundamental importance on making time to enjoy everything that the city has to offer. Parisians work hard, but there is something to be learned from the fact that they rarely race down the street, coffee in hand—coffee is taken sitting down in a café, or standing at a bar. There's a time and a place for everything!

France's central geographical location is reflected in the behavior of its inhabitants. When dreary winter overtakes the capital, Parisians scrunch into their scarves and make like chill-weary northern Europeans. In the summer, when the weather turns balmy and café terraces overflow, the city vibe verges on southern, even Mediterranean. Aside from this climate-dependent shift, Parisians share behavioral characteristics with urbanites the world over. They are active, open-minded, and fully engaged with art and culture.

UNIVERSITY LIFE

Students in Paris are generally unused to the idea of a strong university community that many American students take for granted, because American-style campuses are all but nonexistent. Student infrastructure (in the form of governing bodies, clubs, and associations) seems much less prevalent in France, which can make it challenging to get involved in student life. This is augmented by the fact that while students are concentrated in certain neighborhoods during the day, in the evening everyone goes back to his or her respective nook in the city. On-campus housing is basically nonexistent within Paris city limits, so you won't automatically have a base of peers to socialize with when the day is done.

French students work extremely hard throughout high school to earn their *baccalauréat*. Once they have this in hand, they automatically have the right to enroll in any regular public university. In these state-run institutions, the tuition is negligible by American standards, but the trade-off is disorganization and overcrowding. In general, three years of study at the university level in France is considered equivalent to an American BA, though this always depends on the rigor of the curriculum.

Another option for ambitious French students is to try to pass the extremely competitive entrance exam for admittance to one of the country's prestigious *grandes écoles,* including the École Polytéchnique, the École Normale Supérieure, and the École Nationale d'Administration. These schools are strictly reserved for the cream of the crop, who are either specifically trained or expected to work in the civil service upon finishing their studies.

LIVING ON THE CHEAP

Paris may be beautiful, but that beauty doesn't come cheap. A terrible exchange rate and a higher cost of living make Paris a pretty expensive place. How can you put your wallet at ease? Here are some basic tips to get you started:

- **Student ID:** As a student or young person, you'll have access to numerous discounts all over the city, and you should always carry around your student ID if you have one. Many discounts in Paris are available to both students and young people, usually those under twenty-six (sometimes, twenty-eight). Be sure to ask about student or youth discounts whenever you buy tickets for museums, theater, music, dance performances, or films, or book any travel.

- **International Student ID and Exchange Cards:** An International Student Identity Card (ISIC) or International Student Exchange Card (ISE card) will give you discounts on hostels, restaurants, tours, clubs, and attractions in over 100 countries, as well as access to emergency help-lines, health insurance, and other benefits. Some cards also offer discounts on international phone calls, airfares, and shopping. See www.isecard.com or www.istc.org for de-tails. For nonstudents who are under the age of twenty-six, there is an International Youth Identity Card (IYIC) which offers similar benefits. Visit www.istc.org to see whether you're eligible and how to apply.

- **Rent:** If you have an apartment, rent is an unavoidable cost, but you can potentially get money to offset the expense from the Caisse des Allocations Familiales, which grants rent subsidies to those in need, including foreign students. Visit www.caf.fr for details.

- **Transportation:** If you'll be in Paris for a full year, your best transportation option is to get a yearlong pass called the *carte Imagine'R*, which is reserved for students alone. The added advantage to this pass is that it allows you to travel anywhere in the Île-de-France region on weekends and holidays, so you can explore your surroundings with-out having to worry about breaking the bank. If you'll be in Paris for less than a year, you can invest in a *carte or-ange*, which will run you a little less than €50 a month. For further train travel, get a *Carte 12–25* if you're under twenty-six. It gives you discounts of 25–50 percent on any trip you take. Check out www.12-25-sncf.com for further details.

- **Museums:** Certain museums give reduced entry only to students, others to young people, usually those under twenty-six. If you're an art history student, you have the best deal around: You can get into most museums for free. If you're an English teacher with a *carte professionelle*, the same holds true. However, even with these discounts available, it's often worthwhile to invest in a yearlong pass for a certain museum that you know you'll frequent. For example, for around €20 for a year you can get a youth deal on a *laissez-passer* at the Centre Georges Pompidou, which grants you unlimited visits, entrance to movies at the Centre, and other benefits. Well worth the cost, even if you're in Paris only for a few months.

- **Movies:** Normally, reduced admissions prices at the movies are given to students. Be sure to bring your student ID when you buy tickets!

- **Cultural activities:** For theater, opera, and dance performances, universities often make very cheap tickets available to students. Ask at your student affairs office for details. You can also line up to get last-minute discounted tickets at most performance venues.

- **Food:** Cooking at home rather than eating out is an excellent way to save money. There are enough great food shops and grocery stores to provide you with a cheap and tasty meal. When you just don't feel up to cooking, you can always grab lunch at a *resto U*, or student cafeteria, for mere pocket change.

10 BOOKS AND 10 FILMS TO CHECK OUT BEFORE YOU LEAVE

Once you make the move to Paris, what exactly will you be in for? Only time will tell. But to get a first glimpse of the City of Lights, *and* to get in the Parisian mood, check out these books and films:

BOOKS

1. *Nadja,* André Breton
2. *A Year in the Merde,* Stephen Clarke
3. *Paris to the Moon,* Adam Gopnik
4. *A Tale of Two Cities,* Charles Dickens
5. *A Moveable Feast,* Ernest Hemingway
6. *Les Misérables,* Victor Hugo
7. *Tropic of Cancer,* Henry Miller
8. *Zazie in the Métro,* Raymond Queneau
9. *Me Talk Pretty One Day,* David Sedaris
10. *The Autobiography of Alice B. Toklas,* Gertrude Stein

FILMS

1. *An American in Paris* (1951), Vincente Minnelli
2. *Breathless* (1960), Jean-Luc Godard
3. *Zazie dans le métro* (1960), Louis Malle
4. *La Femme Nikita* (1990), Luc Besson
5. *Les Amants du Pont-Neuf* (1991), Léos Carax
6. *Le Fabuleux Destin d'Amélie Poulain* (2001), Jean-Pierre Jeunet
7. *Moulin Rouge* (2001), Baz Luhrmann
8. *Le Divorce* (2003), James Ivory
9. *Before Sunset* (2004), Richard Linklater
10. *Paris, je t'aime* (2006), numerous directors

1. Paperwork & Practicalities

Y**our life in Paris** will surprise you in ways you can't even imagine—but you'll need to plan certain details ahead of time. The first order of business is getting a passport. If you already have one, make sure it won't expire while you're away. You'll also need to get a student visa. Be sure to apply well before you need both documents, as they can take a month or more to process.

Your university will likely guide you along the way when it comes to your passport and visa applications, but in this chapter, we'll give you a crash course so you know exactly what to expect. Once you've taken care of the nuts and bolts, you can get to the fun parts of life abroad—like figuring out the fastest way to get from Charles de Gaulle to a *pain au chocolat.*

PASSPORTS

If you've never held a U.S. passport, you can apply for one in person at your local passport facility (there are more than 8,000 such passport facilities in the United States). If you're renewing your passport, apply by mail *unless* your most current passport has been damaged, lost, or stolen, or was issued when you were under the age of sixteen (in which case you must apply in person). Standard processing time for passports is six weeks; expedited service, with an extra fee, takes two weeks. Most passports are valid for ten years. You can find all the information you need about applying for a passport, including the location of the nearest passport facility, at www.travel.state.gov.

PASSPORT CHECKLIST

Here's what you need to bring with you when you apply for a passport:

- ✔ Fee payment, which is $97 as of this publication

- ✔ Completed application form (available online)

- ✔ Two identical passport-size photos

- ✔ A birth certificate or other proof of U.S. citizenship

- ✔ A valid photo ID

LOSE YOUR PASSPORT?

If you lose your passport during your time in Paris, head directly to the passport office at the U.S. Embassy in Paris—no appointment is necessary. If your passport expires while you're abroad, you can also renew it through the U.S. Embassy. For more information on dealing with lost passports and other emergencies, see Chapter 18, "Emergencies."

U.S. Embassy in Paris Ⓐ 2 avenue Gabriel 75382, Ⓣ 01 42 66 97 83, Ⓦ http://paris.usembassy. gov, Ⓜ Concorde

---

STUDENT VISAS

You must apply for a visa in person at your local French consulate, which, depending on where you live, could be quite a haul to get to. To ensure that you don't make a long trip in vain, *be as thorough as possible* in putting together your application before-hand. Check your regional consulate's website for information on what documents you'll need to bring with you, as requirements may vary. Applications can take up to six weeks to process. While you're waiting, feel free to inundate the consulate with phone calls and emails—it may help hurry things along. You can find the location of your regional consulate on the website of the French Embassy in the United States, www.ambafrance-us.org.

STUDENT VISA CHECKLIST

Here's what you'll probably need to bring with you when you apply for a student visa:

- ✔ Two completed, signed copies of a long-stay visa application form

- ✔ A valid passport

- ✔ Two passport-size photos

- ✔ A letter of admission from the university in France where you'll be studying

- ✔ A letter from your American university stating that you are currently enrolled as a student

- ✔ Proof of financial guarantee ($600/month minimum income from an outside source or person) or personal income (in the form of a letter of recommendation from your bank with your account information and numbers clearly indicated)

- ✔ The visa fee, approximately $120, payable in cash or by credit card

REGISTERING WITH THE U.S. EMBASSY

It's always a good idea to register your trip with the U.S. Embassy in Paris at https://travel registration.state.gov/ibrs (choose the "long-term traveler" option if you'll be abroad for longer than six months). By providing information about your stay and your emergency contact, you'll help the embassy find you quickly in the case of an emergency back home (or abroad). The embassy can also offer assistance if you're involved in an accident or a crime—see Chapter 18, "Emergencies," for more information.

OTHER TYPES OF VISAS

If you hope to extend your stay after classes end or if you have a nonstudent significant other who will be joining you during your time abroad, there are three other types of visas you should know about:

- **Work visa:** A work visa is required for any non-student who intends to work in France. Work visas are notoriously difficult to get and require that you first find a French employer willing to sponsor you. For more information on work visas, see Chapter 11, "Working."

- **Long-stay visa:** A long-stay visa is required for nonstudents who plan to join their spouse or significant other while they are studying abroad. As a spouse, the only time you won't be required to jump through visa hoops is if your husband or wife has successfully attained a long-term work visa (and not, for example, a one-year post teaching English at a university). Long-stay visas are also required if you simply want to spend more than ninety days in France. No matter what your situation, this type of visa does not allow you to work during your time in France.

- **Tourist visa:** Tourists who are just visiting Paris don't need to worry about visas. The stamp you get in your passport is considered a tourist visa, and it permits you to visit countries in the Schengen area, an open-border zone whose participating countries include Austria, Belgium, Denmark, Finland, France, Germany, Greece, Iceland, Italy, Luxembourg, the Netherlands, Norway, Portugal, and Sweden. You're free to visit up to ninety days over a six-month period, which begins on the day your passport is stamped when you enter Europe. The ninety days do not have to be consecutive, so days you spend outside the Schengen area—for example, for a trip to London or Krakow—don't count against your total. After ninety days, your tourist visa expires and can be renewed only after the six-month period is up.

KEEPING IT LEGAL

If you enter France on a tourist visa and stay longer than ninety days over a six-month period, guess what? You're an illegal alien. When you attempt to leave or reenter France, or should you have a run-in with police, you may be detained, deported, or forced to pay hefty fines.

STUDY-ABROAD CHECKLIST

Before packing your bags and heading to the airport with a big ole' excited grin on your face, make sure you've checked the following off your list:

- ✔ Get a **passport.**

- ✔ Get a **student visa.**

- ✔ Book your **plane ticket.**

- ✔ Arrange **housing,** if it's not already provided for you, or find a hotel/hostel if you plan to do an apartment search once you've arrived in Paris (see Chapter 4, "Finding Housing").

- ✔ Apply for an **International Student Identity Card (ISIC),** which can get you great discounts on travel, entertainment, and more (see "Living on the Cheap" in the Introduction).

- ✔ Set up **online financial statements** and **bill payment.**

- ✔ Arrange for **absentee voting** if you'll be abroad during an election.

- ✔ Schedule a predeparture **physical** if you need one. You don't need to get any particular vaccinations before going to France as long as your routine vaccinations, such as tetanus-diphtheria and measles, are up to date.

- ✔ Get a copy of your **medical records,** especially if you have a preexisting condition for which you'll need treatment abroad.

- ✔ Make sure you have adequate **health insurance** coverage (your university should help with this). See Chapter 9, "Health," for more information about health insurance options and getting medical treatment while in Paris.

- ✔ Set up **VoIP service** with your friends and family so you can keep in touch for free (see Chapter 8, "Staying in Touch").

- ✔ Refill any **prescription drugs** you need. See Chapter 9, "Health," for your options when it comes to buying prescription medications in Paris.

- ✔ Stock up on **over-the-counter-drugs** such as aspirin and cold medicine. Your American drugs will come in handy down the line when you need to restock your medicine cabinet—showing the pharmacist your American product may help him or her find you the French equivalent

- ✔ Make a **photocopy of your passport** and leave it, along with your **contact info** in Paris, with your family.

- ✔ Call your **credit card** companies to inform them you'll be abroad so you don't receive concerned phone calls that someone is using your card overseas.

- ✔ Stock up on **American products** you may not be able to get abroad, such as your favorite brands of deodorant, hair products, or moisturizer.

- ✔ Stock up on **clothes** and other essentials (Paris has the best selection of clothes for sale anywhere on the planet, but you'll find prices to be much higher than in the United States—especially because you'll be paying in euros and sales happen just twice a year).

- ✔ Enough already. Now **get going!**

10 SONGS TO DOWNLOAD FOR YOUR FLIGHT TO PARIS

1. "Le Rendez-Vous," Manu Chao
2. "Paris," Jonatha Brooke
3. "Paris," Elton John
4. "Je t'aime . . . moi non plus," Serge Gainsbourg
5. "April in Paris," Billie Holiday
6. "Paris, Paris," Malcolm McLaren and Catherine Deneuve
7. "Angeliou," Van Morrison
8. "I Love Paris," Peter Cincotti
9. "Give Paris One More Chance," Jonathan Richman
10. "Paris," Delerium

2. The Neighborhoods

Ore than just one monolithic urban entity, Paris is a series of villages, and each area has a distinctive identity, style of resident, and feeling. The city is highly concentrated, so you can put on your walking shoes and get acquainted with the different neighborhoods easily. The twenty *arrondissements* (districts) of Paris spiral outward from the city's geographical and historical heart, around Châtelet and Île de la Cité. The River Seine divides the Right Bank (north) from the Left Bank (south).

Generally, the western half of the city, as well as the heart of the Left Bank, is wealthier and more bourgeois, while east Paris, especially on the Right Bank, contains the traditional working-class districts. These days, however, many of the poorest residents have been pushed outside of the city altogether in the wake of gentrification. Paris is an extremely wealthy city, and while the city's reputation for refinement precedes it, seek out the peripheral areas if you're in search of some of the more authentic neighborhoods. A certain degree of charm and beauty, though not always of the obvious variety, exists just about everywhere in the city.

BEAUBOURG/LES HALLES
1ST/4TH ARRONDISSEMENT
Ⓜ **Châtelet, Les Halles, Étienne Marcel, Rambuteau, Hôtel de Ville**

This area is a hip, artsy magnet for students and tourists alike. It's dominated by the architecturally playful Centre Georges Pompidou, with its preeminent collection of modern and contemporary art, bookstores, an immense public library, cafés, cinemas, and lecture halls. The other neighborhood landmark is the sprawling underground shopping complex of Les Halles, ever convenient, if not always particularly pleasant (it can seem a bit dingy compared with the charm of Paris).

WHAT YOU'LL SEE:

- The whimsical Niki de Saint Phalle–designed **Stravinsky Fountain** by the **Centre Georges Pompidou.** Ⓜ Rambuteau

- The consumer-driven flow of humanity at **Les Halles shopping center.** Ⓜ Les Halles

- The magnificent Gothic façade of the **St-Eustache Cathedral,** completed in 1637. Ⓐ place du Jour 75001, Ⓜ Les Halles

- Henri de Miller's large sculpture of a head, **"L'Écoute,"** in **place René Cassin.** Ⓜ Les Halles

- The eternally-under-scaffolding **St-Jacques Tower at Châtelet,** all that remains of the **Église St-Jacques-de-la-Boucherie,** destroyed in 1797. Ⓜ Châtelet

- The ornate **Hôtel de Ville** (City Hall), rebuilt in the nineteenth century after the original structure was destroyed in a fire. Ⓐ place de l'Hôtel de Ville 75004, Ⓣ 08 20 00 75 75, Ⓦ www.paris.fr, Ⓜ Hôtel de Ville

LOUVRE
1ST ARRONDISSEMENT
Ⓜ **Louvre-Rivoli, Palais Royal-Musée du Louvre, Tuileries, Concorde, Pont-Neuf**

The riches housed within the walls of the astonishing Louvre museum warrant repeated visits, while its extensive gardens and vast courtyards are lovely to stroll through—especially at night, when they're lit up to sublime effect. The surrounding area is quite posh, especially around the infamous place Vendôme, home to the cream of the couture crop.

WHAT YOU'LL SEE:

- I. M. Pei's famous glass pyramid in the courtyard of the **Louvre.** Ⓐ place de la Concorde, 75001, ⓣ 01 40 20 50 50, Ⓦ www.louvre.fr, Ⓜ Palais Royal-Musée du Louvre

- Famous French artist Daniel Buren's striped columns in the courtyard of the **Palais Royal.** Ⓐ place du Palais Royal, Ⓜ Palais Royal-Musée du Louvre

- **Rue de Rivoli,** Paris's main east-west artery. Ⓜ Louvre-Tivoli

- The trendier-than-thou crowd sipping cocktails at **Hôtel Costes** (Ⓐ 239 rue St-Honoré 75001, ⓣ 01 42 44 50 00, Ⓦ www.hotelcostes.com, Ⓜ Concorde) and shopping at **Colette.**

- The 3,300-year-old **Obelisk of Luxor** in **place de la Concorde,** where Louis XVI, Marie-Antoinette, and 2,800 other unfortunate souls were guillotined during the French Revolution. Ⓜ Concorde

- The **Orangerie** (Ⓐ place de la Concorde 75001, ⓣ 01 42 97 48 16, Ⓦ www.rmn.fr, Ⓜ Concorde) and **Jeu de Paume** (Ⓐ 1 place de la Concorde 75001, ⓣ 01 47 03 12 52, Ⓦ www.jeudepaume.org, Ⓜ Concorde) museums in the **Tuileries Gardens.**

LE MARAIS
3ʳᴰ/4ᵀᴴ ARRONDISSEMENT
Ⓜ **St-Paul, Chemin Vert, St-Sébastien Froissart, Bastille, Hôtel de Ville**

This is a charming jumble of tiny streets lined with expensive boutiques, gorgeous apartments, lively cafes and bars, and tree-filled squares and gardens. The neighborhood is gay-friendly, and there is a Jewish section concentrated to the north of the St-Paul Métro station, where you can find delicious falafel, pastries, kebabs, and other Jewish and North African specialties.

WHAT YOU'LL SEE:

- **Place des Vosges,** Paris's oldest public square, home of Victor Hugo's former residence turned museum. Ⓜ St-Paul, Bastille

- The remnants of the fourteenth-century **Paris city wall** constructed by Charles V, visible from **rue Charlemagne.** Ⓜ St-Paul

- Black-clad Orthodox Jews in this, the city's best-known Jewish neighborhood.

- **Musée Picasso.** Ⓐ 5 rue de Thorigny 75003, Ⓣ 01 42 71 25 21, Ⓦ www.musee-picasso.fr, Ⓜ St-Paul, Chemin Vert

- A plethora of boutiques in which the purchase of a single article of clothing could eat up your entire savings.

- Rainbows—this is the center of gay life in Paris.

ÎLE DE LA CITÉ/ÎLE ST-LOUIS
1ˢᵀ/4ᵀᴴ ARRONDISSEMENT
Ⓜ **Cité, Châtelet, Hôtel de Ville, Pont-Marie, Sully Morland**

Many administrative and official buildings are located on Île de la Cité, as well as numerous tourist attractions, including Notre-Dame. To the east, Île St-Louis is more residential and upscale—this is the picture-perfect Paris of the imagination. The banks of either island are ideal for a peaceful stroll.

WHAT YOU'LL SEE:

- **Pont-Neuf,** Paris's oldest bridge. Ⓜ Pont Neuf

- The original **Berthillon ice cream parlor,** reputed to serve the best ice cream in Paris. Ⓐ 31 rue St-Louis-en-l'Île 75004, Ⓣ 01 43 54 31 61, Ⓜ Pont-Marie

- Gloomy former prison **La Conciergerie,** part of the **Palace de Justice** complex. Ⓐ 1 quai de l'Horloge 75001, Ⓣ 01 53 73 78 50, Ⓜ Cité

- The **Sainte-Chapelle,** with its amazing stained glass windows, originally completed in 1248 and rebuilt in the nineteenth century after being sacked by revolutionaries. Ⓐ 4 boulevard du Palais 75001, Ⓣ 01 43 73 78 41, Ⓜ Cité

- A stark monument dedicated to Jews deported during World War II on the eastern tip of Île de la Cité. Ⓐ square de l'Île-de-France 75004, Ⓜ Cité

- **Notre-Dame** and hordes of tourists. Ⓐ place du Parvis Notre-Dame 75004, Ⓣ 01 42 34 56 10, Ⓜ Cité

- The bird and flower market by the **Quai aux Fleurs** on Île de la Cité. Ⓜ Cité

QUARTIER LATIN
5ᵀᴴ ARRONDISSEMENT
Ⓜ St-Michel, Cluny-La Sorbonne, Maubert-Mutualité, place Monge, Cardinal Lemoine, Jussieu, Censier-Daubenton

Lively at all hours of the day and well into the night, the Latin Quarter is the traditional epicenter of student life in Paris. Around St-Michel, you'll find some of the best new and used bookstores in the city. And the concentration of independent movie houses is the stuff of cinephile dreams.

WHAT YOU'LL SEE:

- The stately **Sorbonne.** Ⓐ 12 rue de la Sorbonne 75005, Ⓣ 01 40 46 22 11, Ⓦ www.paris4.sorbonne.fr, Ⓜ Luxembourg, Cluny-La Sorbonne

- The colossal, foreboding **Panthéon,** final resting place of many a great French thinker. Ⓐ place du Panthéon Ⓣ 01 44 32 18 00, Ⓜ Cardinal Lemoine

- The medieval treasure trove that is the **Musée de Cluny.** Ⓐ 6 place Paul Painlevé 75005, Ⓣ 01 53 73 78 16, Ⓦ www. musee-moyenage.fr, Ⓜ Cluny-La Sorbonne, St-Michel

- The **Institut du Monde Arabe.** Ⓐ 1 rue des Fossés Saint-Bernard 75005, Ⓣ 01 40 51 38 38, Ⓦ www.imarabe.org, Ⓜ Sully-Morland

- **Boulevard St-Michel,** the central axis of the Latin Quarter. Ⓜ Luxembourg

ST-GERMAIN-DES-PRÉS/MONTPARNASSE
6ᵀᴴ ARRONDISSEMENT
Ⓜ **St-Germain-des-Prés, Odéon, Rennes, Vavin, Montparnasse-Bienvenue**

Schools dot the streets of St-Germain-des-Prés, as do a handful of cafés that are renowned Parisian institutions, such as Les Deux Magots and Café de Flore. The shopping meccas of boulevard St-Germain and rue de Rennes, as well as the Montparnasse Train Station and Tower (the lone skyscraper in central Paris), make this one of the busiest areas in the city.

WHAT YOU'LL SEE:

- The most revered cafés of Paris, including **Les Deux Magots** (Ⓐ 170 boulevard St-Germain 75006, Ⓣ 01 45 48 55 25, Ⓜ St-Germain-des-Prés) and **Le Café de Flore** (Ⓐ 172 boulevard St-Germain 75006, Ⓣ 01 45 48 55 26, Ⓜ St-Germain-des-Prés)

- **Place du 18 Juin 1940,** the (cleaned-up) Times Square of Paris. Ⓜ Montparnasse-Bienvenüe

- **Le Cimetière du Montparnasse,** where many of France's most beloved artists, writers, and musicians are buried. Ⓐ boulevard Edgar Quinet and rue Froidevaux 75014, Ⓜ Edgar Quinet-Raspail

- The impossibly chic bourgeoisie of the **Left Bank.**

- **Rue de Vaugirard**—the longest street in Paris. Ⓜ Rennes

- **Le Jardin du Luxembourg.** Ⓜ Luxembourg

- The eighteenth-century **Église St-Sulpice,** among the largest churches in Paris. Ⓐ place St-Sulpice 75006, Ⓣ 01 46 33 21 78, Ⓜ St-Sulpice

INVALIDES
7ᵀᴴ ARRONDISSEMENT
Ⓜ **Invalides, Assemblée Nationale, Solferino, Rue du Bac, Varenne, La Tour-Maubourg**

Invalides is a ritzy residential neighborhood that houses several governmental buildings. Some of Paris's most famous cultural landmarks are here, including Napoleon's final resting place under the Invalides dome, in a Russian doll–like tomb containing six coffins; the Musée d'Orsay; and the Eiffel Tower. Tourists are everywhere, and cafés and restaurants are pricier than in other neighborhoods. However, after dark, there's little of interest to do.

WHAT YOU'LL SEE:

- Important governmental buildings, including the **Hôtel Matignon,** the official residence of the Prime Minister of France (Ⓐ 57 rue de Varenne 75007, Ⓣ 01 42 75 80 00, Ⓜ Varenne), and the **Palais Bourbon** (Ⓐ 33 bis quai d'Orsay 75007, Ⓣ 01 40 63 64 08, Ⓜ Assemblée Nationale), home to the National Assembly, and the dark-suited, distinguished men and women who work inside of them.

- The **Musée Rodin.** Ⓐ 77 rue de Varenne 75007, Ⓣ 01 44 18 61 10, Ⓦ www.musee-rodin.fr, Ⓜ Varenne

- **UNESCO headquarters.** Ⓐ 7 place de Fontenoy 75007, Ⓣ 01 45 68 10 60, Ⓜ Ségur

- Hordes of camera-wielding tourists headed for the **Eiffel Tower** (Ⓜ Champ de Mars-Tour Eiffel/Bir Hakeim) and the **Musée d'Orsay** (Ⓐ 1 rue de la Légion d'honneur 75007, Ⓣ 01 40 49 48 14, Ⓦ www.musee-orsay.fr, Ⓜ Solférino/RER Musée d'Orsay).

- The vertical gardens adorning the façade of the **Musée du Quai Branly.** Ⓐ 37 quai Branly 75007, Ⓣ 01 56 61 70 00, Ⓦ www.quaibranly.fr, Ⓜ Iéna/Bir Hakeim

CHAMPS-ÉLYSÉES
8ᵀᴴ ARRONDISSEMENT
Ⓜ Champs-Élysées-Clemenceau, Franklin D. Roosevelt, George V, Charles de Gaulle-Étoile

The Champs-Élysées is the grandest of Paris's grand avenues. These days the area is a consumer's paradise, lined with chain stores and restaurants alongside designer names. There are renowned theaters and museums in the neighborhood, as well as embassies and other official buildings. If you come here to party, prepare to spend accordingly.

WHAT YOU'LL SEE:

- The gigantic flagship **Louis Vuitton store.** Ⓜ Charles de Gaulle-Étoile

- The **Arc de Triomphe.** Ⓣ 01 55 37 73 77, Ⓦ www.monum.fr, Ⓜ Charles de Gaulle-Étoile

- The **Palais de l'Élysée,** the official residence of the French president. Ⓐ corner of rue du Faubourg and avenue de Marigny 75008, Ⓜ Champs-Élysées-Clemenceau

- The traffic of **place de l'Étoile,** which strikes fear into the hearts of pedestrians. Ⓜ Charles de Gaulle-Étoile

- The den of opulence that is the **Hôtel de Crillon.** Ⓐ 10 Place de la Concorde, Ⓣ 01 44 71 15 00, Ⓦ www.crillon.com, Ⓜ Concorde

OPÉRA/GRANDS BOULEVARDS
1ˢᵀ/2ᴺᴰ/9ᵀᴴ ARRONDISSEMENT
Ⓜ **Opéra, Pyramides, Quatre-Septembre, Bourse, Richelieu-Drouot, Havre Caumartin, Chaussée d'Antin-Lafayette**

The ornate nineteenth-century Opéra Garnier, home to the famous Phantom, lends this neighborhood its name, although dance performances currently predominate the entertainment offerings. You'll find the big Parisian department stores here, as well as many bank headquarters and airline companies. Around the Pyramides Métro station lies a Japanese neighborhood, where you can fulfill your all your noodle and sushi cravings.

WHAT YOU'LL SEE:

- The constant daytime hum of the **Quartier Drouot,** with its numerous auction houses, galleries, and dealers. Ⓜ Richelieu-Drouot

- Shoppers toting bags of goods from **Galeries Lafayettes** (Ⓐ 40 boulevard Haussmann 75009, Ⓣ 01 42 82 34 56, Ⓦ www.galerieslafayette.com, Ⓜ Auber/Chaussée) and **Printemps** (Ⓐ 64 boulevard Haussmann 75009, Ⓣ 01 42 82 50 00, Ⓦ www.printemps.com, Ⓜ Havre Caumartin)

- Lunchtime crowds on **rue Sainte-Anne.** Ⓜ Pyramides

- Some of the city's most charming covered passages, such as **Passages Verdeau and Jouffroy.** Ⓜ Richelieu-Drouot

- The **Bourse de Paris,** or stock market. Ⓐ 2 rue de Viarmes, Ⓣ 01 55 65 55 65, Ⓜ Les Halles

- **Sentier,** the garment district. Ⓜ Sentier

- The fashionable types around **rue Montorgueil.** Ⓜ Les Halles, Sentier

RÉPUBLIQUE/CANAL ST-MARTIN
10ᵀᴴ ARRONDISSEMENT
Ⓜ **République, Jacques Bonsergent, Gare de l'Est, Goncourt**

Just steps away from the hectic place de la République, the curved pedestrian bridges and quiet cobblestone banks of the canal St-Martin give this stretch of Paris a quaint, relaxed atmosphere. The neighborhood's many cafés, restaurants, and bars make this a fun destination well into the night.

WHAT YOU'LL SEE:

- **Place de la République,** Paris's protest hub, sometimes filled with noisy protestors supporting their cause. Ⓜ République

- Two of the city's most beautiful train stations, the **Gare du Nord** and **Gare de l'Est.**

- The imposing headquarters of the French Communist Party at **place du Colonel Fabien.** Ⓜ Colonel-Fabien

- Loungers, revelers, and musicians, drinking and people-watching along the **Canal St-Martin.**

- The village-like charm of **place Sainte-Marthe.** Ⓜ Colonel-Fabien

- The hectic **rue du Faubourg du Temple.** Ⓜ Goncourt

BASTILLE/OBERKAMPF

11TH ARRONDISSEMENT

Ⓜ **Bastille, Oberkampf, St-Sébastien Froissart, Parmentier, Charonne**

Bastille and Oberkampf are among Paris's trendier areas, and both have split personalities. You can meander through the numerous narrow, peaceful, residential passages, entirely forgetting your urban surroundings, before stumbling upon one of the many streets saturated with bars and restaurants, which draw hordes of young, hip revelers on nights and weekends.

WHAT YOU'LL SEE:

- The produce and artisan markets of **boulevard Richard Lenoir.** Ⓜ St-Sébastien Froissart

- Paris's traditional furniture-making district, along **rue du Faubourg St-Antoine.** Ⓜ Bastille

- The love-it-or-hate-it façade of the **Opéra Bastille,** inaugurated July 14, 1989, the bicentennial of the storming of the Bastille. Ⓐ 2–6 place de la Bastille 75012, Ⓣ 01 44 61 59 65, Ⓦ www.opera-de-paris.fr, Ⓜ Bastille

- The wholesale clothing district around the Voltaire Métro station.

- Tucked-away, one-of-a-kind clothing boutiques and independent record, video, and book shops.

- International hipster-types on **rue Amelot.** Ⓜ St-Sébastien Froissart

ALIGRE

12TH ARRONDISSEMENT

Ⓜ **Faidherbe-Chaligny, Ledru-Rollin, Reuilly Diderot, Gare de Lyon**

Aligre is a haven for food-lovers. One of the biggest and cheapest open-air markets in the city is held here six days a week, and on the web of streets extending out from place d'Aligre are a number of specialty food stores, in addition to some exceptional restaurants and wine bars.

WHAT YOU'LL SEE:

- **La Liberté,** a left-wing café and neighborhood institution. Ⓐ 196 rue du Faubourg St-Antoine 75012, Ⓣ 01 43 72 11 18, Ⓜ Faidherbe-Chaligny

- The ornate **Gare du Lyon,** built for the 1900 World's Fair.

- Patrons and enthusiastic vendors at the neighborhood's market, **Marche d'Aligre.**

- **Le Pain au Naturel,** one of the city's finest bakeries, just off of place d'Aligre. Ⓐ 5 place d'Aligre 75012, Ⓣ 01 43 45 46 60, Ⓜ Ledru-Rollin

- The elevated **Promenade Plantée,** a former railway heading southeast from the Bastille.

BERCY/BIBLIOTHÈQUE
12ᵀᴴ/13ᵀᴴ ARRONDISSEMENT
Ⓜ **Bercy, Bibliothèque François Mitterrand, Quai de la Gare, Cour St-Émilion**

The Bibliothèque Nationale de France (BNF) and the Bercy complex (which houses, among others, the French Ministry of Finance, the Palais Omnisports stadium, a somewhat Disneyesque "Bercy Village," and a giant multiplex theater) face each other across the Seine in this section of the city, which has undergone extensive renewal and development in recent years.

WHAT YOU'LL SEE:

- The **BNF,** designed to resemble four giant open books. Ⓐ 11 quai François 75013, Ⓣ 01 53 79 53 79, Ⓦ www.bnf.fr, Ⓜ Bibliothèque

- The many galleries of **rue Louise Weiss.** Ⓜ Chevaleret

- **Parc de Bercy,** one of Paris's largest green spaces. Ⓜ Bercy

- **Les Frigos,** an artists' squat housed in a massive former warehouse. Ⓐ 19 rue des Frigos 75013, Ⓣ 01 44 24 96 96, Ⓦ www.les-frigos.com, Ⓜ Bibliothèque

- The Frank Gehry–designed former American Center, which now houses the **Cinémathèque Française.** Ⓐ 51 rue de Bercy 75012, Ⓣ 01 71 19 33 33, Ⓦ www.cinematheque.fr, Ⓜ Bercy

PLACE D'ITALIE/BUTTE AUX CAILLES
13TH ARRONDISSEMENT
Ⓜ **Place d'Italie, Tolbiac, Corvisart, Porte de Choisy**

The area around the place d'Italie is Paris's Chinatown, home to great Asian supermarkets (including the enormous Tang Frères) and some of the best Chinese and Southeast Asian restaurants in the city. The Butte aux Cailles area lies just west, with tree-lined streets and charming houses.

WHAT YOU'LL SEE:

- **L'Hôpital de la Pitié-Salpêtrière,** the largest hospital in Europe. Ⓐ 47–83 boulevard de l'Hôpital 75013, Ⓣ 01 42 16 00 00, Ⓜ Saint-Marcel

- The **Manufacture des Gobelins,** a renowned, centuries-old tapestry-weaving factory. Ⓐ 42 avenue des Gobelins 75013, Ⓣ 01 44 54 19 33, Ⓜ Gobelins

- The high-rises of **place d'Italie,** the antithesis of typical Parisian architecture. Ⓜ Place d'Italie

- The **Gare d'Austerlitz,** completed in 1867.

PLACE DE CLICHY/PIGALLE
9TH/17TH/18TH ARRONDISSEMENT
Ⓜ **Place de Clichy, Blanche, Pigalle**

The sidewalks around place de Clichy and Pigalle are generally jammed with neon lights and diverse crowds.

Along boulevards de Clichy and de Rochechouart, the heart of the somewhat seedy red-light district, there are dozens of sex shops, along with some of the most renowned concert venues in the city. Shops specializing in musical instruments abound to the south.

WHAT YOU'LL SEE:

- Loiterers, voyeurs, and disappointed **Moulin Rouge**–seeking tourists (the reality just doesn't live up to the movie version).

- **Le Cimetière de Montmartre,** where you can pay your respects to famous artists, writers, composers, and other greats—including the likes of Stendhal, Degas, and Truffaut. ⓣ 01 43 87 64 24, Ⓜ Place de Clichy

- An abundance of anglophone pubs for when you need a pint of Guinness—or just a friendly conversation in English.

- The **Musée de la Vie Romantique,** where the spirit of George Sand lingers. Ⓐ 16 rue Chaptal 75009, ⓣ 01 55 31 95 67, Ⓦ www.paris.fr/musees/vie_romantique, Ⓜ Pigalle

- The racy, four-story **Musée de l'Érotisme.** Ⓐ 72 boulevard de Clichy 75018, ⓣ 01 42 58 28 73, Ⓜ Blanche

MONTMARTRE
18ᵀᴴ ARRONDISSEMENT
Ⓜ **Abbesses, Anvers, Lamarck-Caulaincourt, Jules Joffrin**

Montmartre is a true village. The peaceful, hilly streets, adorable façades, and steep staircases make for an ambiance found nowhere else in the city—and only steps away from the tourist frenzy of Sacré-Coeur and place du Tertre. Cozy cafés, chic boutiques, and markets give this village bustle and color.

WHAT YOU'LL SEE:

- **Marché St-Pierre,** where Parisians go for all of their fabric needs. Ⓐ 2 rue Charles Nodier 75018, Ⓣ 01 46 06 92 25, Ⓜ Anvers

- The steep staircases carved into the sides of **Montmartre.**

- The blindingly white curves of **Sacré-Coeur cathedral,** completed in 1919. Ⓐ place du Parvis du Sacré Coeur, Ⓣ 01 53 41 89 00, Ⓦ www.sacre-coeur-montmartre.com, Ⓜ Anvers

- Windmills left over from as far back as the sixteenth century, among Montmartre's most iconic images—one of the most famous windmills sits atop the Moulin Rouge (neon-lit, of course).

- **Abbesses,** the lovely, art nouveau Métro station.

- **The Dalí Museum.** Ⓐ 11 rue Poulbot 75018, Ⓣ 01 42 64 40 10, Ⓦ www.dali-espacemontmartre.com, Ⓜ Abbesses

BARBÈS/CHÂTEAU ROUGE/LA CHAPELLE
10ᵀᴴ/18ᵀᴴ ARRONDISSEMENTS
Ⓜ **Barbès-Rochechouart, Château Rouge, La Chapelle, Gare du Nord**

The pace is frenetic around the clock here, and the area features cheap outdoor markets and stores. You'll find a rich selection of exotic products, owing to the African, Indian, and Sri Lankan communities that make this neighborhood one of the most diverse in Paris.

WHAT YOU'LL SEE:

- Cheap everything at **Émpire Tati,** a discount store with numerous outlets selling everything from clothes to household items to jewelry—look around and you'll find one. Ⓦ www.tati.fr

- Basketball games under the elevated Métro line 2.

- The giant flea market at **Porte de Clignancourt.** Ⓐ avenue de la Porte de Clignancourt, rue Jean-Henri Fabre, Ⓜ Porte de Clignancourt

- The trendy **Ice Kube bar,** a definitive sign of gentrification in this, one of Paris's seedier neighborhoods.
  Ⓐ 1–5 passage Ruelle 75018, Ⓣ 01 42 05 20 00,
  Ⓜ La Chapelle

CANAL DE L'OURCQ/LA VILLETTE
19TH ARRONDISSEMENT
Ⓜ **Stalingrad, Jaurès, Laumière, Ourcq, Porte de Pantin, Corentin Cariou, Porte de la Villette**

The canal de l'Ourcq, the continuation of the canal St-Martin, flows through a decidedly more working-class area. The bars and restaurants are not as prolific, but on a balmy evening, the canal's banks are hopping with picnickers, musicians, and lovers out for a stroll. The canal cuts through the Parc de la Villette, where you can enjoy the open space or attend exhibitions, concerts, circuses, and outdoor movies.

WHAT YOU'LL SEE:

- The chain **MK2 movie theater megaplex.** Ⓐ 14 quai de Seine / 7 quai de Loire 75019, Ⓣ 08 92 68 47 07 / 08 92 69 84 84, Ⓦ http://mk2.fr, Ⓜ Jaurès, Stalingrad

- The vast former municipal funeral parlor, in the process of being converted into a space for contemporary artistic creation called "**104 Aubervilliers.**"
  Ⓐ 104 rue d'Aubervilliers 75018, Ⓜ Riquet

- **Pétanque** (a form of boules) players along **canal de l'Ourcq.** Ⓜ Porte de Pontin

- The giant silver **Géode at la Villette,** where IMAX films are projected. Ⓐ 26 avenue Corentin-Cariou 75019, Ⓣ 01 40 05 81 70, Ⓜ Porte de la Villette

- Peaceful pedestrian bridges.

BUTTES-CHAUMONT/BELLEVILLE
19ᵀᴴ/20ᵀᴴ ARRONDISSEMENT
Ⓜ **Buttes-Chaumont, Belleville, Pyrénées, Botzaris, Place des Fêtes**

Parc des Buttes-Chaumont, with its lush, rolling hills, is a veritable oasis of tranquility and contrasts sharply with the formal French conception of green space. The many delightful sights and smells of Belleville lie just steps away.

WHAT YOU'LL SEE:

- The contrast between the large-scale **place des Fêtes** and the village-like ambience of the adjoining streets. Ⓜ Place des Fêtes

- The endless curves of **rue des Pyrénées.** Ⓜ Pyrénées

- The highest point in Paris, at the **Télégraph Métro station.**

- The lovely houses and flowered gardens of **La Mouzaïa** district.

- **International Belleville,** home to large populations of Arabs, Jews, Africans, and Chinese.

MÉNILMONTANT/PÈRE-LACHAISE
11ᵀᴴ/20ᵀᴴ ARRONDISSEMENT
Ⓜ **Ménilmontant, Père-Lachaise, Couronnes, Rue St-Maur**

The Père-Lachaise cemetery, beautiful and atmospheric, is the largest green space in Paris. It perennially draws tourists seeking out the final resting spots of Jim Morrison, Oscar Wilde, and Edith Piaf, among many others. The surrounding neighborhoods are mainly residential and, to varying degrees, trendy. Endless café terraces line the wide boulevard de Ménilmontant, home to a two-day-a-week open-air market, while the smaller back streets are quite peaceful.

WHAT YOU'LL SEE:

- The tiny alleyways off **rue de Bagnolet** where many former factories have been reconverted into artists' *ateliers,* or studios. Ⓜ Alexandre Dumas

- The steep incline of **rue de Ménilmontant.** Ⓜ Ménilmontant

- The graceful spires of l'**Église Notre-Dame de la Croix.** Ⓐ 2 bis rue Julien Lacroix 75020, ⓣ 01 58 70 07 10, Ⓜ Ménilmontant

- Le **Mur des Fédérés** (Wall of the Federalists) in **Père-Lachaise,** where 147 participants in the Paris Commune were executed on May 28, 1871. Ⓜ Père-Lachaise

- The contemporary glass façade of the **Théâtre National de la Colline at Gambetta.** Ⓐ 15 rue Malte-Brun 75020, ⓣ 01 44 62 52 52, Ⓦ www.colline.fr, Ⓜ Gambetta

5 PLACES WHERE YOU'LL FIND AMERICAN STUDENTS

1. **Coffee Parisien:** Burger- and brunch-seeking Yanks frequent this trendy anglophone spot near St-Germain, just next to the Village Voice Bookshop. Ⓐ 4 rue Princesse 75006, Ⓣ 01 43 54 18 18, Ⓜ Mabillon

2. **The Moosehead:** This bar's soul is Canadian, and the clientele is largely anglophone. Ⓐ 16 rue des Quatres Vents 75006, Ⓣ 01 46 33 77 00, Ⓜ Odéon

3. **Reid Hall:** Go incognito at this academic center in Montparnasse, home to many American universities. Ⓐ 4 rue de Chevreuse 75006, Ⓣ 01 43 20 33 07, Ⓜ Vavin

4. **Tea & Tattered Pages:** English-speakers come to quench their thirst for reading material and tea (and student-friendly prices) at this cozy Left Bank spot. Ⓐ 24 rue Mayet 75006, Ⓣ 01 40 65 94 35, Ⓜ Duroc

5. **Le Violon Dingue:** This Latin Quarter bar hosts a rowdy young American crowd fond of sedentary beer-drinking during the week and basement-dancing on the weekend. Ⓐ 46 rue de la Montagne Sainte-Geneviève 75005, Ⓣ 01 43 25 79 93, Ⓜ Maubert Mutualité

3. Getting Around

The layout of Paris may lead you to question the French's reputed love for all things logical and orderly. One neighborhood's jumble of narrow cobblestone streets and passageways abruptly ends in a chaotic ten-way intersection, while just past this pedestrian nightmare lies one of the many wide, tree-lined boulevards that crisscross the city (the result of Baron Haussmann's attempt to impose order upon the revolution-happy Parisian population in the late nineteenth century).

Paris is fairly small—about forty square miles, compared, for example, to the six hundred square miles of London—so your feet will take you farther than you think. And when the weather isn't cooperative, or when your feet just need a break, one of the world's finest public transportation systems is at your disposal. The Métro and an efficient bus system will get you around the city during the day and evening hours.

Tip
Pick up a copy of the *Plan de Paris*, a handy, pocket-size guide to the city available at bookstores. It contains neighborhood, Métro, and bus maps, plus an index of every Parisian street.

THE MÉTRO

The Paris Métro is efficient, reliable, and reasonably priced. The city's 368 Métro stations are well-lit and well-staffed, and the different stops are generally spaced no more than 300 yards apart. You'll generally find the Métro to be the quickest way around the city.

The Métro begins running around 5:30 A.M. and stops between 12:30 A.M. and 1:00 A.M., depending on the line. So if you plan to party until the wee hours, consider how you'll be getting home. For up-to-date maps and fare information, check out the RATP (Paris Transportation Authority) website, www.ratp.fr.

NAVIGATING THE SYSTEM

There are fourteen main Métro lines that crisscross Paris and extend into the nearest suburbs, as well as two *bis* (secondary) lines, each represented by a different color on the RATP maps posted in- and outside of every station. Each line has either two or three end points, so you must determine the line's end point in the direction in which you are headed. Connecting lines are not announced, but are visible on the line maps displayed throughout the train.

To figure out how to get where you're going and which Métro line to choose, ask yourself three questions:

1. *Where am I going?* Identify the station nearest your destination.

2. *Which line(s) will take me there?* If your starting and ending stations aren't on the same line, change trains where their lines meet on the Métro map.

3. *In which direction am I traveling?* Follow station signs for your desired line and direction. Your direction is the end station you're heading toward on the Métro map. For example, if you want to take line 12, go toward either Mairie d'Issy or Porte de la Chapelle.

BUYING TICKETS

Tickets can be purchased at Métro station counters, machines (available in nearly every station, but which generally only accept coins or European bank cards), or at *tabacs* (tobacco shops) displaying an RATP sign. Tickets are good for both the Métro and buses, and one ticket is valid for one entry with unlimited transfers. Keep your ticket throughout the ride in case RATP inspectors appear—traveling without a valid ticket can lead to a fine. Individual tickets for the Métro are €1.40. A packet of ten, called a *carnet,* is €10.90. The cost per ticket is the same no matter how far in the system you travel.

LONG-TERM PASSES

If you'll be using public transportation regularly, it's smart to invest in a long-term pass. Choose from the following.

La Carte Imagine'R A yearly pass for students. This pass costs €281.30, payable in one installment by check or money order, or in nine monthly installments if you have a French bank account. Applications are available in most Métro stations.

Les cartes oranges These passes allow unlimited transportation for a week (€15.70) or month (€52.50) at a time. Exact cost depends on the zones you plan to travel in.

THE ZONE SYSTEM

Île-de-France is divided into eight concentric transportation zones, comparable to the rings of a dartboard target, with Paris proper, zone 1, as the bull's eye. The farther you go from Paris, the more the fare for the ride. If you're living and studying in Paris, a transportation pass good for zone 1 alone should suit your needs.

BUSES

Dozens of bus lines crisscross Paris, providing reliable, if not always rapid, service. Although the Métro closes down at night, there are about thirty-five night bus lines (*Réseau Noctilien)* that run between 12:30 A.M. and 5:30 A.M., with regular departures to Paris neighborhoods and suburbs scheduled from one of four train stations (Lyon, Est, St-Lazare, and Montparnasse) and place de Châtelet. For all bus information, visit the RATP website.

Each bus line is a different color and is known by its number and end station. The end station is always indicated on the front of the bus, and the line's abridged itinerary, with both end stops and main stops, is often painted on the side. The detailed bus maps located inside every bus shelter will give you the bus's timetable and complete itinerary. Many bus stops have an electronic display that counts down to arrivals and notifies passengers of delays.

BUYING TICKETS

There is no difference between bus and Métro tickets; all Métro tickets and long-term passes are valid for buses and night buses. Tickets can also be purchased on buses and at certain end stations. As with the Métro, the bus system is organized by zones, so you may have to use more than one ticket if you travel more than two zones. Your ticket is not valid for transfers between buses or from the bus to the Métro.

You should board a bus at the front door, closest to the driver, and validate your ticket by inserting it into the validation machine near the front of the bus. Be sure to take your ticket when it pops out and hold onto it throughout your ride because riding without a validated ticket can lead to a fine. If you have a pass, flash it to the driver as you climb on; you don't have to validate it. When you want to get off, press one of the red buttons located throughout the bus to signal to the driver to stop.

TAXIS

While Paris's excellent public transportation normally does the job, taxis are a reasonably priced means of getting from place to place. They are particularly useful as a less crowded, speedier alternative to night buses after the Métro stops running. Taxis circulate throughout the city, and the legitimate ones are recognizable by the *Taxi Parisien* signs atop the vehicles, which are lit up when the taxi is free. In addition to this sign, the taxi must contain a meter indicating the fare and distance of your journey and a visible license number. Most taxis are black, white, or gray.

Taxi stands are prevalent in busy areas throughout the city and can always be found at train stations and in large squares. On Friday and Saturday nights, expect a long wait. If you're not in the vicinity of a taxi stand, you may hail a cab on the street. Otherwise, you can dial a radio-taxi service at 01 47 39 47 39, which will send a driver.

TAXI FARES

The base taxi fare is €2, which increases according to a fixed rate per kilometer (around €0.75–€1.30/km) when the taxi is in motion and according to an hourly rate (around €25–€27/hour) when the taxi is sitting in traffic. These rates are least expensive Monday through Saturday during the day and most expensive mornings, evenings, and Sundays. Pay the driver in cash at the end of the ride. Tipping is not necessary, especially for short trips. However, tips are certainly appreciated: Rounding up to the closest euro is an acceptable rule of thumb.

BIKES

While Paris is not as bike-friendly as other European cities, the city's extensive network of cycling paths is constantly being expanded, and cyclists abound, especially when the weather is nice. Cycling is generally ing and other hazards. A bike could feasibly become your primary mode of transportation in this relatively small, flat city.

There are small independent bike shops all over the city that sell new and used models, parts, and accessories and perform repairs. For a used bike, expect prices to start no lower than €100 for a pretty basic model in good condition. For new bikes, check out Go Sport (www.go-sport.fr), a large chain sporting good store that has several locations throughout the city.

RENTING A BIKE

Paris has numerous bike rental shops. Be ready to provide your passport and a deposit in case something happens to the bike.

Paris à vélo, c'est sympa! Rentals at this shop cost €13 for 12 hours, €17 for 24 hours, €25 for a weekend, and €60 for a week. A deposit of €250 is required. Ⓐ 22 rue Alphonse Baudi 75011, ⓣ 01 48 87 60 01, Ⓦ www.parisvelosympa.com, Ⓜ Richard Lenoir

RATP You can reserve a bike online through the RATP and arrange to pick it up at Les Halles or Bastille. You'll be charged €6 for a night, €10 for a weekday, €22 for five weekdays, €27 for a weekend, and €32 for eight full days. If you have a yearly or monthly public transportation pass, you'll get a 10 percent discount. A €200 deposit is required. Ⓦ www.rouelibre.fr

GENERAL RULES OF THE ROAD FOR CYCLISTS

Here are some key points to keep in mind:

- **Where you can ride:** Stay on the right-hand side of the road. Riding on sidewalks, on park pathways, or in the wrong direction on one-way streets can lead to a fine.

- **Safety:** Talking on your cell phone while riding is prohibited. Always be vigilant when passing parked cars, as people often open their doors without looking first.

- **Required equipment:** Your bike should be equipped with a yellow or white headlight and a red taillight, two functioning brakes, a bell or horn, and pedal reflectors. Bike helmets are strongly recommended.

CARS

As a student or young person, you'll probably have to do very little driving while you're in Paris. Public transportation is more than adequate within the city, and French trains weave an efficient web around the country. If you're set on exploring France or Europe from behind the wheel, however, renting a car is relatively affordable. For more information, see "Renting a Car" in Chapter 17.

GENERAL RULES OF THE ROAD FOR DRIVERS

For the most part, the same rules you'd follow in the United States are applicable in Paris. Here are a few reminders:

- **Speed limits:** General speed limits are 80 kph on the highway, 70 kph on city freeways and on two-lane roads separated by a shoulder, and 55 kph on two-lane roads separated only by a painted line.

- **Safety:** You can be fined for not wearing a seatbelt or for using a hand-held cell phone while driving. In general, driving in Paris is safe for experienced drivers.

TRAINS

To reach the outskirts of Paris and beyond by train, you have two options. The five lines of the RATP-run RER (regional express network) crisscross the region, intersecting with Paris Métro stations at various points within the city. The regional train, the Transilien, which is part of the SNCF (French national railways), stops at five Paris train stations. These two train systems provide an extensive network of public transportation.

RER and Transilien tickets are available at any train or Métro station, either at the counters or from the machines, but not on the trains themselves. Like Métro and bus tickets, they may be purchased in packets of 10. Carte orange and carte imagine'R passes can be used on all RER and Transilien trains, if valid for the applicable zones. One major advantage of the carte imagine'R is that it allows for unlimited travel all over Île-de-France on weekends and holidays, even if only normally good in zone 1 (Paris proper). Your ticket is generally necessary to enter and exit the turnstiles for both RER and Transilien trips and should also be retained in case a controller shows up.

RER When navigating the RER, pay particular attention when determining the terminus station, as many of the lines branch several times. Train platforms have boards that indicate the terminus of the approaching train. You'll find maps, ticket prices, and timetable information on the RATP website. Ⓦ www.ratp.fr

Transilien Consult the timetable board at the station, which will list the train number and terminus and indicate the platform number where you should board. You'll find all information, including schedules and which station you need to go to, on the Transilien website. Ⓦ www.transilien.com

TO AND FROM THE AIRPORTS

There are two main airports in the Parisian region, Roissy-Charles-de-Gaulle (CDG) and Orly. CDG, situated about fifteen miles to the northeast of the city, is the largest airport in France. It is used for both domestic and international flights. Orly is nine miles to the south of Paris and is used primarily for domestic flights and as a link between Paris and the rest of Europe. Check out www.aeroportsdeparis.fr for the most up-to-date information on both airports. You can easily get to and from either airport by using the RER and other public transportation.

TO AND FROM CDG

RER To get to and from CDG between 5 A.M. and midnight, take the RER B (blue line). The airport is located at the line's northern terminus. The ride will take about a half hour, and a one-way ticket will cost you about €8.

Air France Bus The Air France Bus stops at several locations throughout the city (place Charles de Gaulle-Étoile, Porte Maillot, and the Gares de Lyon and Montparnasse) every fifteen minutes between 6 A.M. and 11 P.M., although the hours vary slightly depending on the location. The bus costs €12 for a one-way ride, and reservations are not necessary.

Roissy Bus This bus works on the same principle at the Air France Bus, but stops only at Opéra.

Taxi From the city center, a taxi ride could cost up to €50.

TO AND FROM ORLY

RER Take the RER B to the Antony stop and take the Orly Val automatic Métro correspondence to the Orly West or Orly South terminal, a trip that will take about forty-five minutes and cost you about €9 altogether. Alternatively, you could take the RER C (yellow line) to the Pont-de-Rungis-Aéroport d'Orly stop, and from there, take a free shuttle bus to the terminals. This is slightly cheaper, at around €6, but may take longer.

Orlybus Take the Orlybus from the Denfert-Rochereau RER stop. The bus runs every ten to fifteen minutes between 6 A.M. and 11 P.M.. A one-way ticket costs €6.

Air France Bus The Air France Bus picks up at Porte d'Orléans, Gare Montparnasse, Duroc, and Gare des Invalides every fifteen minutes between 6 A.M. and 11 A.M. and costs €8 one way.

Public Bus #285 The cheapest option, #285 runs to and from Orly approximately every thirty minutes. You can pick it up at the Villejuif Métro station.

Taxi A taxi from the city center will cost up to €35.

TRAVELERS WITH DISABILITIES

Unfortunately, getting around Paris can be particularly challenging for those with disabilities. Cars reign supreme, uneven cobblestone streets and narrow sidewalks abound, and elevators big enough to accommodate wheelchairs are a rarity. Check out the RATP website, www.ratp.fr, and www.infomobi.com for more specifics about transportation in Paris and www.parisinfo.com/guide_paris for information about all aspects of everyday life for people with disabilities.

5 THINGS THAT MAKE YOU THINK, "NOW THAT'S PARIS"

1. **Haughty service:** You'll find plenty of exceptions to this rule in Paris, but don't be surprised when your entry into a shop yields no more than a raised eyebrow, or when you speak perfectly comprehensible French at a café and are still given dramatically puzzled looks from the waiter. It's all part of Paris.

2. **Modern technology:** We're not sure what the deal is with the rolled-up carpets that gently facilitate the flow of water streaming out of the city's sewers, but it's kind of charming, and very Paris. You'll see them *everywhere,* so keep your eyes open.

3. **High-heeled, skirted women on bikes:** This odds-defying combination is carried off with the greatest of ease and elegance by *les Parisiennes*.

4. **Covered passages:** Charm reaches new heights when pavement turns into tile and a glass ceiling separates you from the sky. The most extensive networks of Parisian passages, including the Galerie Vivienne and Passages Jouffroy and Verdeau, are in the 2nd and 9th *arrondissements*, near the Palais Royal and Métro Richelieu-Drouot.

5. **All that is *not* Paris:** The outside influences, the foreign-born inhabitants, and the international cultural centers, clubs, and cafés all create a diversity that defines the city.

4. Finding Housing

Getting an apartment in Paris is a prospect both thrilling and daunting. A studio is probably the most common living situation for students and young people in Paris. Studios run the gamut from the shoebox-size former maids' quarters found on the top floor of every old Parisian building, to spacious artist's lofts that rent for more than some one-bedroom apartments.

Housing offers abound in the fall, but because that's when students return from summer vacations, be prepared for ferocious competition. You'll often have to fight doubly hard as a foreigner, unless you manage to find a place via word of mouth. You may have to adjust your notions of living space to get used to that sixth-floor walk-up, shower in the kitchen, or shared hallway toilet (or other hallmarks of student life in Paris). Sometimes, what Paris apartments lack in modern amenities are more than made up for in charm and character.

APARTMENT LISTINGS

The cheapest way to find an apartment in Paris is to do it without the help of a broker or third-party agent. Be quick in responding to ads, and don't shy away from being persistent or making early morning phone calls. Online listings tend to be more up-to-date and useful; search print publications only when they are hot off the press.

Particuliers à Particuliers, which appears every Thursday, is the holy grail of apartment listings. Wake up at the crack of dawn to pick it up at the newsstand and start placing those calls to sleepy landlords. The online version of the paper is www.pap.fr, which is updated several times daily. You can also check out websites such as www.appartement.org and www.colocation.fr, which charge small fees for access to renters' contact information.

Craigslist Paris (http://paris.craigslist.org) can be a good resource. Keep in mind, however, that websites and publications geared toward Americans in Paris, such as FUSAC (www.fusac.fr), often list apartments with inflated rents. Alternatively, consult the ads posted at the American Church (www.acparis.org) often geared toward students, or on the bulletin boards at universities and municipal libraries.

APARTMENT HUNTING TIPS

Here are a few key points to keep in mind during your apartment search:

- As a student, you'll most likely need a financial guarantor who resides in France. This doesn't have to be a parent or relative. If you have a friend who works and is willing to take legal responsibility for you (on paper, at least), this will do.

- Bring a checklist with you when you visit prospective apartments. Be sure to check for things such as storage space, electrical outlets, water pressure, whether you can hear noise from the street or neighboring apartments, and whether appliances such as the refrigerator and stove are in working order.

- If the apartment needs repairs (repainting, fixing leaky pipes or faulty wiring), ask the landlord to take care of this as soon as possible, preferably before you move in. If you're in a hurry to move in, be sure to get a written confirmation from the agency of the work that will be performed.

APARTMENT LISTING LEXICON

What Americans think of as the first floor is called the ground floor or *rez-de-chaussée* in France (the "0" or "RDC" button in the elevator). Up one flight of stairs is the first floor (*1er étage*), up two flights of stairs is the second floor (*2ème étage*), and so. Here are some other common terms you'll find in apartment ads (the French don't tend to use abbreviations):

caution	deposit
chambre de bonne	former maid's quarters
charges comprises	utilities included
chauffage collectif	centralized heating
chauffage électrique individuel	individual electric heating
colocation	apartment share
courte/longue durée	short/long-term
cuisine équipée	equipped kitchen
cuisinette	kitchenette
douche + WC	separate shower and toilet ("water closet")
garanties demandées	guarantor required
location	rental
meublé/non-meublé	furnished/unfurnished
refait à neuf	renovated
salle de douche/salle d'eau/salle de bain	bathroom with shower and toilet together
sous-location	sublet

BROKERS

Enlisting the services of a broker can take a lot of the headache out of your apartment hunt. While private landlords can verge on hysteria when it comes to the amount of paperwork they require, apartment agencies are aware of all the legal logistics and tend to be more reasonable when it comes to documentation. In addition, apartment rents are often better regulated through agencies, and thus a bit lower than those charged by individual landlords. The catch, of course, is that whatever savings you may incur on rent are balanced out by the fact that you'll have to pay a broker's fee, usually equivalent to one month's rent.

To find potential brokers, stroll down the street to drool over the apartment ads on display in agency windows throughout the city. Or check out websites such as www.avendrealouer.fr and www.seloger.fr to search agency rental listings. To access agency contact information on the most recent listings, you'll have to pay a small fee. Another benefit of using a broker is time. Agency rentals are not necessarily snapped up as quickly as private rentals.

APARTMENT PRICES

Be prepared to pay three months' rent before moving in: the first month's rent plus a security deposit equivalent to two months' rent. The security deposit will be refunded upon your departure, assuming you leave the place in decent condition. If you go through an agency, the broker's fee is added on top of this, bringing the total to four months' rent up front—and sometimes more. In general, living in a *collocation* (with roommates) tends to be more reasonable than living alone, and you can easily find ads for rooms that rent for well under €500 per month. You'll avoid a broker's fee, and you can often negotiate how much money you must pay up front.

Studios are generally more popular with young people than apartments with roommates. An acceptable price for a 9 m² *chambre de bonne,* the cheapest (and most claustrophobic) option, is €300 at most.

A more spacious studio of 15–20 m^2 normally rents for €400–€600. A one-bedroom apartment can go for €700–€1,000.

To offset these elevated rents, everyone, including foreigners with residency permits valid for more than four months, can benefit from a state housing subsidy known as the CAF (Caisse d'Allocations Familiale). Depending on your rent and resources, you may be granted up to half of your total rent per month. For more details and to download an application, go to www.caf.fr.

LOCATION, LOCATION, LOCATION

The neighborhoods most popular with young Parisians are mainly concentrated on the eastern half of the Right Bank, which is patronized by a crowd that's more bohemian than bourgeois—but with money to burn. Accordingly, the low rents that originally attracted artists and young people have inflated with the times. Rents listed are per month.

- Bastille/Oberkampf: studio, €400–€800; one bedroom, €700–€1,100
- Le Marais: studio, €500–€900; one bedroom, €800–€1,300
- Ménilmontant/Père-Lachaise: studio, €400–€700; one bedroom, €650–€1,00
- Montmartre: studio, €450–€750; one bedroom, €700–€1,200
- République/Canal St-Martin: studio, €400–€800; one bedroom, €700–€1,100

LEASES

You may be forced to make a fast decision when looking at an apartment, as there is rarely any shortage of potential renters. Do not, however, sign a lease or hand over any money if you have lingering doubts. Once you sign a lease, you'll have a difficult time getting out of your obligations or being reimbursed. Always ask for written confirmation of any sum of money you have paid and to whom you have paid it, along with the person's address and phone number.

If you don't rent an apartment through an agency, be aware that it's common practice for landlords to rent out apartments under the table to avoid paying taxes. If this is the case, you'll have no official lease. However, you need formal housing documentation to carry out your life in Paris, such as opening a bank account and getting a phone. If this is your situation, ask for a letter from your landlord attesting to your occupancy. You should also get photocopies of his or her French national identity card and of the most recent utility bills from the apartment.

UNDERSTANDING LEASES

You'll almost always sign a lease for a one-year period. Expect a standard lease to include the following information:

- The rental period and starting date.

- The amount of rent, when it's due, how it is to be paid, and the terms of rent increase (the rent can be hiked every time a new contract is drawn up).

- Whether you can leave before the end of the lease and the procedure for giving notice. It's common to have a break clause, which allows the tenant to give notice after a certain period of time. Generally, you can give your landlord three months' notice if you wish to leave an apartment before your lease is up.

- The apartment furnishings and equipment shared by the building's tenants (heating, elevator, garbage containers, intercom). Usually, an inventory is conducted at the beginning and end of tenancy to document the exact state of the apartment and its contents. The inventory is used to assess damages when the tenancy concludes.

- Who is responsible for repairs.

- Amount of the security deposit, which is limited to two months' rent. The deposit will either be held by the landlord or the company that manages the property.

HOMESTAYS

A homestay is a semester- or yearlong arrangement in which you live with a French family—typically with your own bedroom, a bathroom that may or may not be shared, and two meals a day. The advantage of a homestay is that it forces you to immerse yourself in language and culture, something that is difficult to do if you're living in a studio apartment or a student residence. In exchange, however, you may compromise some degree of independence and privacy.

Before deciding whether a homestay is for you, be careful to assess your eating preferences. Meals can be hit or miss depending on your host's culinary skills (and your level of pickiness). Refusing meals may create friction in the household. And because board is included in the price, you'll wind up paying double if you feel the need to eat out frequently. If you have any dietary restrictions, such as vegetarianism or allergies, you might need more control over meal preparation than homestays allow.

If you'd like to pursue a homestay, discuss this option with your school. Your program might be able to match you with a French family, or you can try combing apartment listings for homestay notices. Families will often advertise rooms specifically intended for young international students. These will be listed under the "shared" ads (*partagé* or *collocation*). Rates vary depending on the specific accommodations that you or your school arrange.

5 PARIS APARTMENT QUIRKS

1. **Nonexistent ovens:** When space is lacking, as it often is in Parisian apartments, you may have to make do with a single hotplate.

2. **"Heaters":** It's electric, warms the part of your body that's pressed up against its surface, and causes you to choke upon receiving your utility bill. Unfortunately, this variety of heater is the norm in many old buildings in Paris.

3. **Teeeeeeeeny-tiny bathrooms:** By American standards, everything is smaller in France. If you need evidence, look no further than your apartment's bathroom.

4. **Turkish toilets:** If you live in a *chambre de bonne* (former maid's room), you may share with your hallmates a *toilette à la turque*—a toilet that is nothing more than a hole in the floor. But this is actually much more sanitary than your standard sit-down basin!

5. **Rule-bending:** You may be surprised at the poor condition of many apartments when you visit or move in. Landlords often take advantage of the ferocious competition for housing, knowing that tenants will line up regardless of the peeling paint, water stains, and leaky plumbing.

5. Shopping

Shopping is serious business in France, and grocery shopping may be one of the most pleasant pursuits of your stay in Paris. If you're a gastronomic amateur looking to cultivate your cooking skills, Parisian markets will provide you plenty of inspiration and ingredients. Superior-quality food is easily accessible—and a good deal less expensive than in the United States. The fruits and vegetables available in France are tastier and more beautiful than the produce sold in American markets. Meat, fish, and dairy products are fresher, and the bread and pastries are a deliciously distant relative of what we call carbohydrates back home.

And for non-food-related shopping, Paris will not disappoint even if you're on the tightest of student budgets. You may be tempted to browse at one of Paris's high-end department stores or pop into a few cool boutiques as you make your way around town. But to maximize your purchasing power, head straight to one of Paris's excellent flea markets. In all cases, there are countless treasures in store when you set out to shop in Paris.

SUPERMARKETS

In typical supermarkets, you'll find almost any food product you want, from frozen pizzas to foie gras, though items are sometimes sold in smaller quantities and devoid of the excessive packaging that American consumers may be used to. The dairy aisle in your average supermarket surpasses anything you'll find in the United States, and you'll find everything from Roquefort to the plastic-wrapped, orange cheese product we all know and love. Supermarkets are generally open from 9:00 A.M. to anywhere between 8:00 P.M. and 10:00 P.M. Monday through Saturday.

In general, food prices are comparable to those in the United States (though with the weak dollar, anything priced in euros will be more expensive for Americans than it would be otherwise). Two major exceptions are cheese and yogurt, which are much cheaper in France than in the United States. Delicious fresh bread from France has no American grocery store equivalent—and you'll pay as low as €0.40 for a baguette!

Check out these budget supermarket chains, branches of which you'll find all over Paris.

Atac and Franprix These two chains have a slightly more limited selection than Monoprix, but they still carry an extensive range of goods. Ⓦ www.atac.fr and www.franprix.fr

---

Ed and Leader Price Both are popular discount chains. Ⓦ www.ed-fr.com and www.leader-price-int.com

---

Monoprix Monoprix offers an excellent selection of products and carries several lines of its own brands, including organic and gourmet foods. Some branches have butchers, bakers, and dairy counters. Ⓦ www.monoprix.fr

---

GROCERY SHOPPING 101

Keep these tips in mind when you're heading out to the grocery aisles:

- **Understanding quantities:** Most French products are labeled according to the metric system. Take note of these conversions: 1 kg = about 2.2 lbs; 100 g = about 3.5 oz; and 1 L = about 2.1 pints.

- **Buying milk:** In addition to the more expensive selection in the refrigerated section, you may be surprised to find unrefrigerated milk in square cartons and plastic jugs in the aisles. Shelf-stable milk can be stored at room temperature until opened, when it must be refrigerated.

- **Buying produce:** In many supermarkets, you must weigh your own produce. Place your selection on the scale located in the produce department and press the corresponding button, and a sticker with the weight and price will come out.

SPECIALTY FOODS

If you have the time and the inclination, try shopping in the French tradition: stopping at a half-dozen small specialty shops to pick up the individual ingredients. The merchants at these shops are happy to offer advice on food selection or preparation, making for a far more personal shopping experience.

BAKERIES

Forget all the impostor baguettes you've eaten before coming to France and get ready for the real deal. The pleasure of exiting a *boulangerie* (bakery) clutching a fresh-from-the-oven loaf of bread is immeasurable, one of the true highlights of living in Paris. Every neighborhood has at least one bakery, and many bakeries have a specialty baguette that—as you'll soon see—tastes different from any other baguette you've ever sunk your teeth into. Keep in mind that boulangeries sell bread and baked goods; for your more extravagant, sweet-toothed inclinations, *pâtisseries* (cake shops) specialize in cakes and pastries.

CHEESE SHOPS

Your enjoyment of French cheeses is directly proportional to your ability to withstand pungent odors. If you don't wrinkle your nose at them, you'll have the opportunity to enjoy the infinite array of cheeses produced in every nook and cranny of the country. The *fromagerie,* or cheese shop, is a sacred—and smelly—institution, generally offering a core array of cheeses in addition to a varying selection of more unusual, geographically diverse samplings. When in doubt about what to buy, ask the *fromager* (cheesemonger).

SAY CHEESE!

A soft, ripe *camembert* can be quite tasty, or you might consider trying a hard, flavorful *comté.* If you're enticed by the smellier side of the spectrum, try a *livarot* or a *munster* (a far cry from the shiny orange-and-white slices you get back home). On the safer side, try a *morbier,* with its interior line of ash, or a creamy *brebis. Chèvre* can run the gamut from a soft, mild log to a shriveled, dry, sharply flavored round. Also be sure to sample the queen of blue cheeses, *Roquefort.*

PRODUCE SHOPS

Produce shops in Paris are a kind of compromise between supermarkets and farmers' markets. The produce can be of decent, good, or exceptional quality, and prices vary accordingly. Different shops play by different rules, although it's a sign that you're in good hands if there are employees who select the fruits and vegetables for you, as they can pick and choose with a professional eye.

BUTCHERS

Every neighborhood in Paris has its share of butcher shops. There are also *volaille* (shops specializing only in poultry). In addition, horsemeat, a not-unheard-of delicacy in France, is sold at certain Parisian butchers, who usually hang a gold or plastic horse's head over their shop's entrance. *Bouchers* (butchers) also often carry an assortment of sausages, pâtés, and other organ-specific specialties. Prices may be slightly higher than at a grocery store, but the selection and service more than compensate.

FARMERS' MARKETS

Going to Parisian farmers' markets is an ever-enjoyable activity and a pastime in itself. The market is a social hub, a continually bustling village of tarps and tables manned by the same familiar faces, week in and week out. This is where you'll find some of the best produce France has to offer, as well as meats, dairy products, and all of your other culinary or household needs.

Markets are open anywhere from two to six days a week, generally including Friday, Saturday, or Sunday, when Parisians stock up for weekend feasts. Markets usually open early in the morning: Trucks can arrive as early as 4:00 A.M., and things will be hopping by 6:30 A.M. On the weekend, the activity can last well into the afternoon, sometimes ending around 3:00 P.M. During the week, vendors will finish packing up closer to 1:30 P.M. or 2:00 P.M. There are also a handful of markets open on Wednesday afternoons, from 3:00 P.M. to 8:00 P.M. Here are a few of the most well known.

Marché d'Aligre This is one of the largest and most animated markets in Paris, open every day except Monday. Weekends, when the crowds are thick and the vendors are shouting over one another for your attention, you may think you're in a Moroccan casbah rather than Paris. Ⓐplace d'Aligre, 75012, ⓂLedru Rollin

Marché Barbès The Marché Barbès is open Wednesdays and Sundays. This is one of the cheapest markets in Paris, and because it is located in an ever-bustling African and Arab neighborhood, exotic offerings are available. Ⓐboulevard de la Chapelle, 75018, ⓂBarbès-Rochechouart

Marché Belleville This market, which morphs into the Marché Père-Lachaise further south, occurs Tuesdays and Fridays and is always busy. The neighborhood's incredible diversity makes for a vast array of unusual edible offerings. Ⓐboulevard de Belleville, 75011, ⓂBelleville

Marché Place des Fêtes This large market takes place under the modern high-rises of northeast Paris, where the air is nicer and you'll find fewer tourists. It's open Tuesdays, Fridays, and Sundays. Ⓐplace des Fêtes, 75019, ⓂPlace des Fêtes

Marché Raspail This market is open Tuesdays, Fridays, and Sundays. On Sundays, it's reserved for organic agricultural vendors, making it one of only three organic markets in Paris. Ⓐboulevard Raspail, 75006, ⓂRennes

SPECIAL DIETS

There are many *biologique,* or just *bio* (organic), super-markets in Paris, including the chain Naturalia, that offer a wide array of vegetarian and vegan products. To find more information about vegetarian and vegan stores and restaurants in Paris and throughout Europe, go to www.happycow.net. If you keep kosher, there are many Jewish enclaves in Paris where you can find kosher supermarkets and restaurants. Some notable spots are in the Marais, around rue des Rosiers, and in many parts of the 11th, 19th, and 20th *arrondissements.*

Here are a few well-known specialty supermarkets, all of which charge in the same price range as regular supermarkets.

Bio Génération Aligre An independent organic grocer in the food-focused Aligre neighborhood. Prices are slightly higher than at Naturalia, but every six months you will receive a voucher for 10 percent of the total you've spent during that time. Ⓐ 34 rue d'Aligre 75012, Ⓣ 01 43 42 53 23, Ⓦ www.bonneterre.fr, Ⓜ Faidherbe-Chaligny

Cacher Price A smaller independent kosher grocery store selling strictly kosher products at slightly elevated prices, although the store always offers special deals on a changing array of items. Ⓐ 39 rue Merlin 75011, Ⓣ 01 47 00 75 28, Ⓦ www.cacher-price.fr, Ⓜ Père Lachaise

Franprix Cacher A kosher branch of the mid-priced Franprix supermarket, offering a large selection of products at reasonable prices. Ⓐ 240 boulevard Voltaire 75011, Ⓣ 01 43 70 90 68, Ⓦ www.franprix.fr, Ⓜ Rue des Boulets

Naturalia The biggest organic supermarket chain in Paris, offering a variety of vegetarian, vegan, and organic products. Online shopping is available through its website. Ⓐ 11/13 rue Montorgeuil 75001, Ⓣ 01 55 80 77 81, Ⓦ www.naturalia.fr, Ⓜ Les Halles

ONE-STOP SHOPPING

Hypermarchés, vast stores selling groceries, clothing, electronics, appliances, and more under one roof, exist only on the outskirts of Paris and are practical only if you have access to a car. However, the chain Monoprix can be found throughout the city. Additionally, the more expansive Inno, owned by the same company, has a few branches within Paris. When looking for an all-in-one shopping experience, these are the names to watch for.

Auchan Ⓐ Centre Commercial Les 4 Temps, parvis de la Défense 92800 Puteaux, Ⓣ 01 41 02 30 30, Ⓦ www.auchan.fr, Ⓜ La Défense

Carrefour Ⓐ 1/3 avenue du Général Sarrail 75016, Ⓣ 01 40 71 33 00, Ⓦ www.carrefour.fr, Ⓜ Porte d'Auteuil

E. Leclerc Ⓐ Centre Commercial Verpantin, 19 rue du Pré St-Gervais 93500 Pantin, Ⓣ 01 48 91 88 04, Ⓦ www. e-leclerc.com, Ⓜ Hoche

Inno Ⓐ 31 rue du Départ 75014, Ⓣ 01 43 20 64 90, Ⓦ www.monoprix.fr, Ⓜ Montparnasse-Bienvenue

Monoprix Ⓐ 15 boulevard St-Denis 75002, Ⓣ 01 42 33 73 52, Ⓦ www.monoprix.fr, Ⓜ Strasbourg-St-Denis

DEPARTMENT STORES

Parisian *grands magasins,* or department stores, are a spectacular (and sometimes spectacularly expensive) attraction for tourists and locals alike. Two ultra-high-end fashion megacomplexes are the dueling Printemps and Galeries Lafayette on boulevard Haussmann. Le Bon Marché, arguably the oldest and most famous department store in the world, is located on the Left Bank, and Le Drugstore, the chic, state-of-the-art shopping and dining complex, is just steps from the Arc de Triomphe. More wallet-friendly shopping centers include BHV and Tati, the Parisian bargain basement. Here's a selection of the most popular Parisian department stores.

BHV (Bazar de l'Hôtel de Ville) Ⓐ 52/64 rue de Rivoli 75004, Ⓣ 01 42 74 90 00, Ⓦ www.bhv.fr, Ⓜ Hôtel de Ville

Le Bon Marché Ⓐ 24 rue de Sévres 75007, Ⓣ 01 44 39 80 00, Ⓦ www.lebonmarche.fr, Ⓜ Sèvres-Babylone

Le Drugstore Ⓐ133 avenue des Champs-Elysées 75008,
Ⓣ01 44 43 79 00, Ⓦwww.publicisdrugstore.com,
ⓂCharles de Gaulle-Étoile, Georges V

Galeries Lafayette Ⓐ40 boulevard Haussmann 75009,
Ⓣ01 42 82 34 56, Ⓦwww.galerieslafayette.com,
ⓂChaussée-d'Antin, Opéra, Havre-Caumartin

Printemps Ⓐ64 boulevard Haussmann 75009,
Ⓣ01 42 82 57 87, Ⓦdepartmentstoreparis.printemps.com,
ⓂHavre-Caumartin, Opéra; RER Auber

La Samaritaine Ⓐ19 rue de la Monnaie 75001,
Ⓣ01 40 41 20 20, Ⓦwww.lasamaritaine.com, ⓂLouvre,
Châtelet, Pont Neuf; RERChâtelet-Les Halles

Tati Various locations. Ⓐ4 boulevard Rochechouart 75018,
Ⓣ01 42 55 13 09, ⓂBarbès-Rochechouart; Ⓐ106 rue
Faubourg du Temple 75011, Ⓣ01 43 57 92 80, ⓂBelleville;
Ⓐ76 avenue Clichy, 75017, Ⓣ01 58 22 28 90, Ⓦwww.tati.fr,
ⓂLa Fourche

HIGH-TRAFFIC SHOPPING AREAS

Part of the fun of living in Paris is discovering the
amazing shops that seem to lurk around every corner
and getting to know the unique stores that are closest
to your home or school. If you're in the mood for a
shopping spree, head to one of these neighborhoods,
each of which offers a staggering shopping selection.

Quartier Latin Home to the Sorbonne, this neighborhood
boasts some of Paris's best (French) bookstores—
including the many yellow awnings of Paris book institution
Gibert Jeune—and the legendary English-language
Shakespeare & Co. ⓂSt-Michel, Cluny-La Sorbonne,
Maubert-Mutualité, place Monge, Cardinal Lemoine,
Jussieu, Censier-Daubenton

Le Marais For funky and eclectic boutique shopping, Le
Marais's wares include pricey clothing, accessories, and
antiques. ⓂSt-Paul, Chemin Vert, St-Sébastien Froissart,
Bastille, Hôtel de Ville

St-Germain Along this stretch on the Left Bank, shoppers find chichi designer boutiques, gift shops, antique stores, and book stores. Ⓜ St-Germain-des-Prés, Mabillon, Odéon

Triangle d'Or The hub of haute couture in Paris, these streets are lined with the likes of Valentino, Louis Vuitton, Christian Dior, Yves Saint Laurent, and Chanel. Ⓜ Franklin D Roosevelt, Alma Marceau

FLEA MARKETS

There are several large *marché aux puces* (flea markets) held near Paris's city limits on the weekends, where you can find new and used clothes, antiques, furniture, CDs, bicycles, and a wide range of other goods. It can be a lot of fun simply to wander around on a Sunday morning, taking in the hustle and bustle. If you're on the hunt for something in particular, head out early and stay focused, or you may come home with an armload of unplanned purchases. Here are some of the best flea markets in the city.

Puces de Clignancourt Saturday, Sunday, Monday 7:00 A.M. to 7:00 P.M. Ⓐ avenue de la Porte de Clignancourt, rue Jean-Henri Fabre, Ⓜ Porte de Clignancourt

Puces de Montreuil Saturday, Sunday, Monday 7:00 A.M. to 5:00 P.M. Ⓐ avenue de la Porte de Montreuil, Ⓜ Porte de Montreuil

Puces de St-Ouen Different antiques dealers have different hours. Information Center: Ⓐ 154 rue des Rosiers, St-Ouen, Ⓜ Porte de Clignancourt

Puces de Vanves Saturday, Sunday 7:00 A.M. to 7:30 P.M. Ⓐ avenue de la Porte de Vanves and rue Marc Sangnier, Ⓜ Porte de Vanves

HOME FURNISHINGS

If you need to pick up some essential items or if you just want to change your décor, you can furnish your place by shopping at the following places.

Emmaüs Emmaüs is a kind of French Salvation Army, where you can find cheap used furniture with character. However, you'll have to go to the branches located outside of the city to access this veritable treasure trove. Visit the website for store locations. Ⓦ www.emmaus.fr

Ikea There are no less than six Ikeas in the Paris region to take care of all your furniture needs. Four are accessible via public transportation. Find the location nearest you on the Ikea website. Ⓦ www.ikea.com.

5 GREAT GIFTS TO SEND PEOPLE BACK HOME

1. **Carambars:** Anyone with a sweet tooth will appreciate these classic French bonbons—but the silly jokes you'll find inside every wrapper might be a bit harder on the stomach.

2. **Chocolate:** The chocolate you'll find in French supermarkets will turn you off of American chocolate forever. No need to spend a fortune—the brand Côte d'Or is inexpensive, and utterly delicious.

3. **Flavored syrups:** The French love to dilute mint, cherry, lemon, or lavender syrup in their Perrier, beer, and wine—an innovation that certainly deserves to be brought back to the United States.

4. **Herbes de Provence:** Send the flavor of Provence to the kitchens of your friends and family. Herbes de Provence is a mixture containing thyme, rosemary, lavender, basil, majoram, and other herbs. A spoonful or two are often used in soups or when cooking meats or other dishes.

5. **Street art:** Send friends a handmade glimpse of what they're missing. For cheap(ish) art featuring gauzy watercolor scenes of nighttime Paris or splashy oil renditions of its famous landmarks, hit up any of the city's countless street artists. The boulevard St-Germain-des-Prés and the squares in Montmartre are good places to browse.

6. Daily Living

L earning to navigate the ins and outs of daily life is part of the game when you're assimilating to any new city. Skills that you take for granted, such as how to do laundry, handle money matters, and mail packages, will suddenly seem new and perplexing. Factor in the language barrier, and even the simplest tasks will become enormous—and often comical—new challenges.

When you deal with service institutions in Paris, one major cultural difference makes itself apparent: In the United States, people generally go out of their way to accommodate you; in France, although politeness and formality are de rigueur, friendliness is definitely not. Knowing what to expect when it comes to daily needs should give you a head start and allow you to jump right into the daily grind.

GETTING MONEY

Before you leave home, set up your U.S. bank and credit card accounts to make them easier to manage from outside the country. Make a point of signing up for online banking and electronic bill payment. Notify your debit- and credit-card providers that you'll be using your cards overseas. Finally, find out how to deposit checks by mail, because you won't be able to make deposits to U.S. bank accounts from Parisian ATMs.

GETTING CASH FROM HOME

The fastest and most economical way to get cash from home is to withdraw it from your U.S. account through an ATM. However, also keep in mind the following options:

- **Cash advance on your credit card:** To do this, you'll need to make sure you have a PIN number before you leave the United States. Be warned: Interest rates can exceed 25 percent.

- **Cashing U.S. checks:** As a general rule, it's best not to have U.S. checks mailed to you, as you'll have a difficult time finding a bank in Paris that will cash them. Even if a bank agrees to cash it, it can take four to six weeks for the check to go through. Another check-cashing option is to see if any of the many exchange bureaus around town are willing to help.

- **International money transfers:** If you have a French bank account, you can have money transferred into your account through an international money transfer. This can take up to forty-eight hours, and a moderate-to-steep fee is usually charged.

- **Western Union or American Express:** You'll receive money quickly—within an hour—using either of these services, but the fees are exorbitant. For the nearest locations in Paris, check out www.westernunion.com or www.americanexpress.com.

- **Wiring money:** This isn't a good choice if you need money quickly. You can arrange to have money wired to you from your U.S. bank; both the sending and receiving banks charge fees, and the transfer can take up to ten business days or longer.

HOW TO USE FRENCH ATMS

French ATMs are simple to use. You can select to do your transaction in English, and then just follow the instructions on the screen, entering your four-digit PIN. If your PIN is longer than four digits, check with your U.S. bank about having it shortened or verify that it will work overseas. The keypads on French ATMs have numbers only, so if you've memorized a word as your PIN, make sure you figure out its numeric equivalent before going to Paris. While you're abroad, keep an eye on your bank balance. Most U.S. banks place daily (and often weekly) limits on withdrawals, and they also charge fees for transactions and for currency conversions. Ask your bank for details.

CHANGING MONEY

Unfortunately for U.S. travelers, the euro has been worth more than the dollar in recent years. The exchange rate fluctuates constantly, but the cost may vary from about $1.15 to $1.45 for €1 (you can easily locate the current exchange rate with a quick online search). If you're on a tight budget, check daily and wait until the rate is as favorable as possible before withdrawing or exchanging a large sum of money. Using an ATM to withdraw cash is your best bet for getting a good exchange rate. Here are some other options for exchanging dollars for euros or vice versa.

- **Banks:** Banque de France changes foreign currencies free of charge, while most other banks will perform these transactions for a small commission.

- **Airports:** You'll notice exchange booths at airports, both when you leave the United States and when you arrive in Paris. Generally, these booths offer very unfavorable rates.

- **Exchange counters:** Currency-conversion kiosks are located at train stations and in touristy neighborhoods (you'll usually see signs in English with the word *Exchange*); expect to be charged a high commission.

6. DAILY LIVING

> **CREDIT CARDS**
>
> MasterCard and Visa are widely accepted in France. If you're an American Express user, bring a back-up card because Amex is not consistently recognized in Europe. Before you leave the United States, call your credit card companies and let them know you'll be abroad (to prevent false alarms about fraudulent charges and the accompanying hassle of frozen accounts). Also ask about what fees you may be charged for overseas transactions; the industry standard is a 2 to 3 percent finance charge.

FRENCH BANK ACCOUNTS

It might be possible to get by without opening a bank account in Paris—at least for a short period of time (six months or less). But if you'll be living in France for longer than that, opening a French bank account is probably a good idea. Having a local account is necessary if you want to sign up for a French cell phone plan (see "Cell Phones" in Chapter 8). And if you plan to live on your own in an apartment, you'll need a local account to pay your utilities (see "Apartment Living"). Having a French account also allows you to deposit checks in euros and to avoid charges assessed by U.S. banks for overseas transactions.

OPENING AN ACCOUNT

Your school may have a partnership with a specific bank—an option definitely worth considering. If you need to select a bank on your own, you'll find that basic accounts vary little from one bank to another. Many banks offer youth advantages for people under twenty-five years old. Choose a bank that's near where you live or study. Although you can make withdrawals and deposits at any branch of your bank, all paperwork must be performed at your home bank, which is the bank where you open your account. French ATMs that allow you to make deposits are not widespread, so you'll probably have to go to the bank counter in person during business hours. Here are some of the most popular banks in Paris; call or check their websites to find the nearest locations.

- **BNP** ℡ 08 20 82 00 01, Ⓦ www.bnpparisbas.net
- **Le Crédit Lyonnais** ℡ 08 20 82 36 89, Ⓦ www.lcl.fr
- **Société Générale** ℡ 01 44 76 57 00,
  Ⓦ www.societegenerale.fr

ACCOUNT CHECKLIST

Bring the following with you when you apply to open a French bank account:

✔ Passport

✔ Student visa or residency permit (if you have one)

✔ Proof of address (either a utility bill or written attestation from your landlord)

✔ Student card

✔ Birth certificate

USING FRENCH CHECKS

You'll use French checks with about the same frequency that you're used to back home—meaning probably not often. But French checks are important to have for paying rent and any medical expenses. They are accepted in nearly all stores, restaurants, and cafés and must be accompanied by an official photo ID, such as your passport. Subscriptions, telephone/Internet expenses, and utilities are generally automatically deducted from your bank account monthly or bimonthly, rather than paid by check.

POSTAL SERVICES

The French postal system is efficient and reliable. There are several post offices located in each *arrondissement,* and your address will link to one particular branch, where you'll have to go to pick up any packages sent to you. With the exception of the post office located on rue du Louvre in the 1st *arrondissement,* which is open twenty-four hours, the branches are generally open 8:00 A.M. to 6:00 P.M. Monday through Friday, and 8:00 A.M. to 12:00 P.M. Saturday. French post offices offer the following different services; for details on locations and hours, visit www.laposte.net.

Sending packages abroad Packages of up to 30 kg (about 66 lbs) may be sent overseas. €15–€276 will guarantee that your package is delivered within four to eight days, package tracking included. €14.50–€197.50 will get your package there in nine to fifteen days, without tracking.

Registered mail You may have to send a *lettre recommandée* (via registered mail), whether it's to end a subscription or a phone/Internet plan. Expect to pay anywhere from €2 to €12 for proof of delivery.

Email Free email accounts are available. Go to ⓦ www. laposte.net/inscription for details.

Bank accounts Bank accounts are available to qualified applicants who are twenty-five or younger. See ⓦ www.bagoo.com for details.

Ready-to-post mail *Prêt-à-poster* (prestamped) envelopes are available in four sizes. For ten regular-size (20 g) envelopes valid only in France, you'll pay about €6. For international mail, you'll pay about €8.40. A letter mailed to the United States takes around seven to ten days to arrive.

EXPRESS DELIVERY

If you need to get a package home fast, the following overseas shipping services are available:

- **DHL** Ⓐ 6 rue des Colonnes 75002, Ⓣ 08 20 20 25 25, ⓦ www.dhl.fr, Ⓜ Opéra
- **FedEx** Ⓐ 63 boulevard Haussmann 75008, Ⓣ 01 40 06 90 16, ⓦ www.fedex.com/fr, Ⓜ St-Lazare

APARTMENT LIVING

As is the case back home, living in an apartment on your own presents many pleasures—along with many responsibilities. You'll have to deal with utilities, which sometimes are already added into your rent by your landlord. In general, electricity and gas consumption is calculated bimonthly, so you'll receive your main utility bills at regular intervals six times a year. Guard these carefully, as they'll serve as proof of address when you deal with bureaucracies. Here's a quick overview of utilities, services, and other day-in/day-out practicalities that are part and parcel of apartment living.

UTILITIES

- **Cable/Television:** There's no charge for basic cable, although in France there is an annual tax of about €100 just for owning a television, which your landlord may or may not take care of. Basic cable provides six stations. If you want more options, you can subscribe to satellite television providers such as Canal+ or TPS. Both offer in the range of 300 channels for about €30 per month. You can subscribe online at www.canalplus.fr or www.tps.fr; you will be charged a monthly fee to rent the equipment, which will be shipped to you. For a guide to France's television stations, see "TV and Radio" in Chapter 7.

- **Electricity:** Your electricity bill will fluctuate depending on the size of your apartment, how it is equipped, and what season it is. In winter, your costs may nearly double, especially if you have electric heating rather than centralized heating. Unfortunately, most old Parisian apartment buildings are badly insulated and have electric heating. You can sign up for service at your local agency or with Électricite de France online at www.edf.fr.

- **Gas:** You're more likely to find electric heating and hotplates in Paris apartments than gas. When you move into your new apartment, the gas may or may not already be functioning; check with your landlord. Whatever the case, you must contact your nearest Gaz de France agency (find locations at http://monagence.gazdefrance.fr) to open a new contract and have a technician come to start up the gas for you.

- **Internet:** If you want to get Internet service hooked up in your apartment, you'll first need to get a landline (see "Telephones" for details). Most high-speed Internet subscriptions provide you with a modem that also sets up digital television and provides free unlimited phone calls within France. The most popular service providers are Free (www.free.fr), Club Internet (www.clubinternet.fr), Neuf (www.neuf.fr), Noos (www.noos.fr), and Orange (www.orange.fr/internet). Shop around to find the best deal.

- **Telephones:** As is the case in the United States, you can easily get by in Paris without a landline. However, landlines are imperative if you want Internet service at home, and they're a good idea if you know you'll be placing a lot of long-distance phone calls—calling from landlines gets you more reasonable rates than calling from cell phones (see "Calling Home" in Chapter 8). Your landline service will most likely be provided by France Télécom, the state phone company (find the nearest branch at www.france-telecom.fr). A basic plan will cost you about €15 a month, plus whatever phone calls you make (domestic calls within France will run you anywhere between €0.03 and €0.09 per minute). There are also a few private companies that offer long-distance plans, including Cegetal (www.cegetel.fr), Télé 2 (www.tele2.fr), and 9 Télécom (www.neuf.fr). Shop around to find the best deal.

FREE

A popular and budget-savvy alternative to France Télécom is to subscribe to Internet service with Free, which cuts your ties to France Télécom (and exempts you from its €15 monthly landline fee) and allows you to place unlimited calls to domestic and international fixed lines for no extra cost. Go to www.free.fr for more information.

SERVICES

- **Garbage:** Use the trash bins made of green plastic with green lids. Depending on your *arrondissement*, your trash will be collected either in the morning between 6:00 A.M. and 12:00 P.M. or in the evening, between 5:00 P.M. and 11:00 P.M. Your building's concierge is responsible for taking trash bins out to the sidewalk for pickup. Go to www.laposte.net/inscription for details.

- **Laundry and dry cleaning:** You'll find *laveries automatiques* (laundromats) and dry cleaners all around Paris. A load of laundry should cost about €3 or €4. For ten minutes of drying time, you'll be charged anywhere from €0.50 to €0.80. Laundromats in Paris accept cash only—and many are equipped to handle only coins. Full-service (drop-off) laundromats are not common in Paris, outside of hotels.

- **Locksmiths:** If you find yourself locked out of your apartment, a *serrurier* (locksmith) can help, although this may cost you up to a few hundred euros. There are locksmiths in every neighborhood, and you'll often receive flyers advertising their services in your mailbox.

- **Maintenance:** The rent for your apartment will include basic maintenance fees for the upkeep of facilities such as elevators and collective electricity, water, and heating. For minor work, such as repairing the plumbing or replacing window glass, call a repairperson yourself and ask for a detailed *facture* (receipt), which you'll need to get reimbursed by your landlord or insurance company. For more extensive work, first get an estimate to give to your landlord to allow him or her to decide how to proceed.

- **Recycling:** For paper, cardboard, and plastic recyclables, use the recycling bins made of green plastic with yellow lids; these are collected twice a week. For glass, use the bins made of green plastic with white lids; these are collected once a week. It's possible that your building will not be equipped to recycle glass. If this is the case, leave your glass recyclables in the large, green, circular depositories located on many street corners.

PRACTICALITIES

- **Apartment insurance:** Apartments in Paris must be insured, either by you or your landlord, against possible damage due to water, fire, theft, or other incidents. Talk with your landlord about the setup for your apartment. Many banks offer advantageous insurance packages for students and young people.

- **Converters and adaptors:** In France, as in most European countries, the standard voltage is 220–240 volts (compared to a standard of 110–120 volts in the United States), and plugs are shaped differently. If you want to bring (and use) your favorite hair dryer or other electric device from home, you'll need to buy a plug adaptor or voltage adaptor/converter. Plug adaptors do not convert electricity but will allow dual-voltage appliances (such as most laptops) to be plugged in. Voltage adaptors/converters are used with small electric appliances (such as hair dryers) intended for short periods of use, and voltage transformers are used with larger appliances such as CD players or TVs—these are sold in kits in the United States for about $30.

5 CHEAP ADVENTURES IN PARIS

1. **Explore abandoned railroad tracks:** For a Parisian path less traveled, walk the abandoned tracks of the Petite Ceinture, a train that used to make the rounds in Paris before it went out of service in the 1930s. The tracks are accessible from different points around town. Ⓜ Porte de Vincennes, Maison Blanche, Porte de Vanves, Porte de Versailles, Balard, Ourcq, Maraîchers, Porte de Montreuil

2. **Visit the Parc de Bagatelle:** Located in the Bois de Vincennes, this park features a beautiful floral garden and eighteenth-century château. Ⓐ allée de Longchamp, Bois de Boulogne 75016, Ⓜ Pont de Neuilly

3. **Tour Paris by bicycle:** See Paris as you never have, on blocked-off streets with a pack of cyclists a few hundred strong. A group called Paris Rando Velo organizes Friday night bicycle tours, complete with volunteer tour guides. The tours depart from l'Hôtel de Ville (City Hall) at 10:00 on Friday nights. Ⓐ place de Hôtel de Ville 75004, Ⓦ www.parisrandovelo.com, Ⓜ Hotel des Ville

4. **Head down to the sewers:** Explore the city's danker side. The sewers of Paris are open for exploration and are more fascinating (and less odorific) than you'd imagine. The entrance is at Ⓐ 93 quai d'Orsay 75007, Ⓣ 01 47 05 10 29, Ⓜ Pont de l'Alma

5. **Ride a city bus:** Forget the expensive tour buses—pick a city bus line and ride it to the end. The scenic line 69 passes some major landmarks, while line 26 runs the length of the lovely, curving rue des Pyrénées, which spans fantastic neighborhoods.

7. Studying & Staying Informed

You'll find no shortage of quiet spots in Paris where you can concentrate while still feeling like you're part of the city. The free and user-friendly public libraries sprinkled throughout every *arrondissement* warrant exploration, and you'll find a host of other options as well.

The city's many independent bookstores are stocked with titles and publications on every subject under the sun, specializing in everything from esotericism to erotica. And though the cries of "New York Herald Tribune!" on the Champs Élysées have long since died down, English-language reading material is prevalent in Paris, including in several English-language bookstores.

PLACES TO STUDY

From cozy cafés to aesthetically inspiring libraries and lovely parks, you'll find nooks and crannies in all corners of the city fit for working. You'll discover your own favorite spots as you get to know Paris, but in the meantime, here are a few to seek out.

Bibliothèque de la Maison de la Culture de Japon This library is part of the sleek, modern Japanese cultural center. How can you be stressed out with all that Zen? Ⓐ 101 bis quai Branly 75015, Ⓣ 0144 37 95 50, Ⓦ www.mcjp.asso.fr, Ⓜ Bir-Hakeim

Bibliothèque de la Maison Européenne de la Photographie This decade-old library is attached to the renowned photography museum. Check out the photos when you need a study break. Ⓐ 5–7 rue de Fourcy 75004, Ⓣ 01 44 78 75 00, Ⓦ www.mep-fr.org, Ⓜ St-Paul

Bibliothèque Forney This is one of the city's most beautiful libraries, devoted to art history. Pull up a chair and prepare to be inspired. Further details can be found under the heading *bibliothèques spécialisées* on the website of the Mairie de Paris. Ⓐ 1 rue du Figuier 75004, Ⓣ 01 42 78 14 60, Ⓦ www.paris.fr Ⓜ Pont Marie

Bibliothèque Nationale Site Richelieu Formerly the principal site of the national library, the Richelieu site contains very lovely reading rooms. Ⓐ 58 rue de Richelieu 75002, Ⓣ 01 53 79 81 26, Ⓦ www.bnf.fr, Ⓜ Bourse

Bibliothèque Publique d'Information The vast library of the Centre Georges Pompidou is one the city's most popular places for studying, a fact to which the queue will attest. There's also a café across the airy lobby if you need some refueling. Ⓐ 19 rue Beaubourg 75004, Ⓣ 01 44 78 12 33, Ⓦ www.centrepompidou.fr, Ⓜ Rambuteau

Centre Culturel Suédois The cozy café here is calm, tucked away, and perfect for studying during the week. Ⓐ 11 rue Payenne 75003, Ⓣ 01 44 78 80 20, Ⓦ www.si.se, Ⓜ Chemin Vert

Cinémathèque de Paris This is the film-focused library of the recently moved Cinémathèque Française. It's particularly good for students of cinema, or for anyone seeking a modern study space. Ⓐ 51 rue de Bercy 75012, Ⓣ 01 71 19 33 33, Ⓦ www.cinemathequefrancaise.com, Ⓜ Bercy

Parc des Buttes-Chaumont Stretch out on one of this park's sprawling lawns. Ⓜ Botzaris, Buttes-Chaumont

Parc Montsouris This park has the advantage of being just next to the Cité Internationale Universitaire, so the student vibe is strong. Ⓜ Porte d'Orléans

Place des Vosges In one of Paris's most idyllic spots, you can seek study inspiration from Victor Hugo, who lived here. Find a shady spot on a bench and ignore the tourists. Ⓜ Bastille

LIBRARIES

Be forewarned that certain French libraries can be a bureaucratic nightmare, seemingly doing everything in their power to make access to knowledge all but impossible. At the national library, Bibliothèque Nationale de France (BNF), you may have to show research credentials to get in the door and, once you're there, sit in an assigned seat, wait patiently while librarians fetch books for you, or follow obligingly as they accompany you through the stacks.

Bibliothèque Nationale de France Ⓐ 11 quai François 75013, Ⓣ 01 53 79 59 59, Ⓦ www.bnf.fr, Ⓜ Bibliothèque

MUNICIPAL LIBRARIES

Want to branch out? Take advantage of the nearly sixty municipal libraries found all over Paris. It's easy to get a municipal library card. Go to any branch with your passport or French national ID card, if you have one, and ask for an application. You'll normally receive your card while you wait, and it is valid for one year. Following is just a short selection of municipal library branches. For a complete list, visit www.paris.fr.

Bibliothèque André Malraux Ⓐ 78 boulevard Raspail 75006, Ⓣ 01 45 44 53 85, Ⓜ Rennes

Bibliothèque Baudoyer Ⓐ 2 place Baudoyer 75004, Ⓣ 01 48 87 49 88, Ⓜ Hôtel de Ville

Bibliothèque Château d'Eau Ⓐ 72 rue du Faubourg St-Martin 75010, Ⓣ 01 53 72 11 75, Ⓜ République

Médiathèque Musicale de Paris Ⓐ Forum des Halles, Porte St-Eustache 75001, Ⓣ 01 42 33 20 50, Ⓜ Les Halles

THE AMERICAN LIBRARY IN PARIS

For a wide selection of English-language books and audio visual materials, visit the **American Library in Paris.** It offers comfortable places to study, wi-fi access, and a variety of cultural events. Apply for a short-term membership (six months) for €65—or inquire about student memberships. Ⓐ 10 rue du Général-Camou 75007, Ⓣ 01 53 59 12 60, Ⓦ www.americanlibraryinparis.org, Ⓜ École Militaire, Alma-Marceau

ENGLISH-LANGUAGE BOOKSTORES

English-language bookstores have been havens for Paris's anglophone writers for generations. These shops, where you can browse and chat for hours, are community-oriented and far from impersonal. They often display want ads, sponsor literary events such as speakers and conferences, and (at least in the case of Shakespeare & Company) offer places to sleep. Here are some of the best English-language bookstores in Paris.

Attica This multilanguage bookstore has a huge collection of pedagogic material and is a great resource for teachers. Ⓐ 106 boulevard Richard Lenoir 75011, Ⓣ 01 49 29 27 31, Ⓦ www.attica.fr, Ⓜ St-Ambroise

The Red Wheelbarrow Its vast collection of literature concentrated into a Paris-size space, this friendly bookstore welcomes a continual flow of local and international authors for readings and talks. Ⓐ 22 rue St-Paul 75004, Ⓣ 01 48 04 75 08, Ⓦ www.theredwheelbarrow.com, Ⓜ St-Paul

Shakespeare & Company This reincarnation of the historic Left Bank institution is a veritable treasure trove of titles old and new, and a meeting place for Paris's anglophone community. Ⓐ 37 rue de la Bûcherie 75005, Ⓣ 01 43 25 40 93, Ⓦ www.shakespeareco.org, Ⓜ Maubert-Mutualité

Village Voice Bookshop This shop has been a beloved haven for the English-speaking community in Paris, readers and writers alike, for nearly a quarter century. Ⓐ 6 rue Princesse 75006, Ⓣ 01 46 33 36 47, Ⓦ www.villagevoicebookshop.com, Ⓜ Mabillon

W.H. Smith The Paris branch of this British chain has one of the largest selections of English-language titles and periodicals in the city. Ⓐ 248 rue de Rivoli 75001, Ⓣ 01 44 77 88 99, Ⓦ www.whsmith.fr, Ⓜ Concorde

NEWSPAPERS

From the dense and intellectual *Le Monde* (www. lemonde.fr) to the communist *L'Humanité* (www.

humanite.presse.fr) to the satirical *Le Canard Enchaîné* (www.canardenchaine.com), newspapers are big business in Paris. In addition to these publications, which are available at newsstands for around €1, there are lighter, free publications, such as *Métro* (www.metrofrance.com) and *20 Minutes* (www.20minutes.fr), available at the entrance of many Métro and train stations. These contain local and international news as well.

NEWSPAPERS IN ENGLISH

If you're aching for an English-language newspaper, your best bet is to check out the online version of your favorite American newspaper. *The International Herald Tribune* (www.iht.com) is also available at any newsstand. It's owned by the New York Times Company and publishes many articles and features taken directly from that paper. You can also find *USA Today* at many newsstands, and many British newspapers are available, including *The Times, The Financial Times, The Daily Mail,* and *The Daily Telegraph.*

MAGAZINES

When you think of French magazines, one word likely comes instantly to mind: *fashion.* Indeed, fashion magazines are a staple of the French magazine diet, and many come with names you'll recognize from home, such as *Vogue* and *Elle.* The clothes and accessories may be just as outlandish, but you'll also find sexy photos and ads that would never be published in the magazines' American counterparts.

You'll also find many free, cultural, English-language magazines, such as *Paris Voice* (www.parisvoice.com) and *Fusac* (www.fusac.fr), that are published regularly and are a good source of information about different events going on around town. *Pariscope* is a weekly publication in French that includes a brief listings section in English called *TimeOut Paris* in the back of each issue. You'll find hundreds of French-language magazines, but the following are worth noting.

Courrier International A weekly publication consisting of articles taken from hundreds of different newspapers, magazines, periodicals, and websites worldwide, which are translated into French and cover a huge variety of topics. The general focus is current events. Ⓦ www.courrierinternational.com

Le Monde Diplomatique A highly respected, independently minded monthly publication dealing with international relations, published in more than twenty different languages worldwide. Ⓦ www.monde-diplomatique.fr

Le Nouvel Observateur A weekly title covering international and domestic current events in all domains, from news and politics to science and technology. Ⓦ http://tempsreel.nouvelobs.com

Les Inrockuptibles A weekly magazine that covers much of the same cultural territory as *Télérama* but with more of a focus on music. Ⓦ www.lesinrocks.com

Paris-Match A weekly magazine, founded in 1949, known for its photos of celebrities, as well as for its good coverage of international news and current events. Ⓦ www.parismatch.com

Télérama A thorough and intelligent weekly source of information on film, literature, music, art, shops, restaurants, and diverse happenings around town. Ⓦ www.telerama.fr

Vogue The French version of the fashion bible, chock-full of all the latest runway fashions (which you just might see on the Paris streets!) Ⓦ http://vogue.fr

TV AND RADIO

Watching French TV is a great way to improve your language skills and get a window into the French soul, although much of what you'll find to watch are dubbed versions of American shows and movies. Instead of watching last season's *Desperate Housewives,* try seeking out news and cultural programs to get a distinctly French perspective on what's happening in the world. Here's a selection of some of France's most popular TV and radio stations.

TFI, TF2, TF3, and TF4 These basic cable TV offerings broadcast a mixed bag of news and dubbed series and movies.

Arte (Channel 5) This joint Franco-German TV station has a consistently interesting international and cultural lineup and is the only one of the basic stations to show nondubbed films and programs.

M6 Home to French reality television.

Canal+ This TV station shows a good selection of subtitled films, football matches, and a wide variety of news and talk shows, but it goes fuzzy much of the time for nonsubscribers.

France Info (105.5) Your best source on the radio for up-to-the-minute information on local, national, and international news. ⓦ www.radiofrance.fr/chaines/france-info/accueil/

France Inter (87.8) This radio station primarily broadcasts talk shows with different daily or weekly guests, interspersed with musical programs and domestic and world news flashes. ⓦ www.radiofrance.fr/franceinter/accueil/

Radio France International (89.0) This radio station has a worldwide focus, with a particular slant on Africa. ⓦ www.rfi.fr

FIP (105.1) This radio station plays an eclectic mix of commercial-free music, day and night. ⓦ www.radiofrance.fr/chaines/fip/accueil

TSF (89.9) This is an excellent jazz radio station. ⓦ www.tsfjazz.com

Nova (101.5) This station ffers mainly electronic and hip-hop music. ⓦ www.novaplanet.com

Radio France The French public radio association has several different stations, each with its own identity. As a global entity, it makes up a sort of large-scale NPR. ⓦ www.radiofrance.fr

5 GOOD EXCUSES NOT TO STUDY

1. **A sunny day:** Get yourself outside and seize this wonderful opportunity. Stroll along canal St-Martin, play Frisbee on l'Esplanade des Invalides, or smell the flowers in Bercy Park.

2. **Language immersion:** Any French language teacher will tell you that the only way to speak French better is to practice, practice, practice. Consider your café-sitting an academic activity: You'll learn more from talking to the locals than from doing your homework, right?

3. **Protests:** If it's Saturday afternoon, chances are there's a protest going on at place de la République concerning immigrants, interns, Israel, or any number of other issues, domestic and international. Go observe an integral part of French culture.

4. **Free admission to the Louvre:** The Louvre, home to the Venus de Milo, the Mona Lisa, and countless other priceless works of art, offers free admission on the first Sunday of the month. Ⓐ Situated between the Seine and rue de Rivoli, and from rue du Louvre to place de la Concorde 75001, ⓣ 01 40 20 50 50, ⓦ www.louvre.fr, Ⓜ Palais Royal-Musée du Louvre

5. **Hunger:** Fresh *baguettes* ... delicious cheeses ... amazing *pastries* ... Hunger is always a good excuse to ditch the books—and never a problem for long in Paris!

8. Staying in Touch

One of the most difficult aspects about moving to Paris is being separated from family and friends. While homesickness is a normal part of studying abroad, luckily there are loads of opportunities to stay connected in real time to those near and dear to you. The Internet, with instant messaging and emailing, is the easiest and cheapest option. In fact, after a few weeks, you'll probably find yourself on a first-name basis with the proprietor of your neighborhood Internet café.

As in most places in the world, cell phones are ubiquitous in Paris, and many who land in Paris—even for short stays—find that getting set up with a French phone and service is essential to feeling connected and truly a part of city life. You may be disappointed to find that Paris is not as plugged in as most American and many other European cities, and the city's café culture has yet to attract a computer-toting clientele. Even in a bar or restaurant that offers free wireless, the server may look at you with trepidation and ask you to sit at the bar when you pull out your laptop. Nonetheless, you'll have no trouble staying in touch while in Paris.

THE INTERNET

The easiest way to get online is probably through your university's computer lab. If you live in university housing, your dorm or apartment might be hooked up as well. When the computer labs are too crowded, you'll find Internet cafés all over Paris. Internet cafés usually charge between €2 and €3 for thirty minutes; you'll generally be charged by the hour or half hour. Try out a few different places until you find one with agreeable rates and a good atmosphere. Unfortunately, Paris lags behind other cities as far as offering free wi-fi in public places. While it's plentiful in the American chains like Starbucks and McDonald's around town, you probably won't encounter too much of it Parisian cafés. Two reliable places to find it are the Centre Georges Pompidou and outside at place Georges Pompidou. For an Internet café that offers especially cheap rates and is open around the clock, visit easyEverything.

---

easyEverything Ⓐ 31/37 boulevard de Sébastopol 75002, Ⓜ Châtelet-Les Halles, Ⓦ www.easyeverything.com

---

CELL PHONES

With rare exceptions, cell phones purchased in the United States won't work in Europe. If you want to use a cell phone during your stay in Paris, you'll almost certainly need to buy a French cell phone and investigate the area's various options for service.

USING SIM CARDS

Pay-as-you-go SIM (subscriber identity module) cards are the best option if you'll be in Paris for a short time. With these prepaid microchips, you don't have to sign a contract with a cellular provider; you just slip the card (smaller than a postage stamp) into your phone and buy blocks of minutes as you need them. Available in denominations starting at about €25, the cards are sold at cell-phone stores, newsstands and various other places all around Paris. They can be recharged with additional minutes as necessary. To use SIM cards, you'll need to purchase a French cell phone, except in the rare case that your U.S. phone is SIM compatible (see "Using Your U.S. Cell Phone" later in this chapter).

> **WATCH YOUR PHONE!**
>
> The fact that SIM cards will work on any phone makes cell phones one of the most commonly stolen items in Paris. Leaving yours on a café table, in a see-through pocket of your knapsack, or even in your hand while walking down a busy street is a risk. On the other hand, SIM cards also mean that should your phone break, your address book will be intact.

SIGNING A CONTRACT

Signing up with a French service provider is the most affordable option if you plan to stay in Paris for a long time. Normally, contracts require commitments of at least one year. There are only three French service providers, all of which offer comparable rates. Do some serious comparison shopping to find the best deal, and be sure to find out whether your university offers special deals with a certain company. Your plan will often include options such as unlimited calls to a set number of friends who use the same provider, unlimited evening/weekend calls, or unlimited text messaging. When you sign a contract, a cell phone may come free with your service or at a low cost. Here are your service provider options.

Tip
If you choose to buy a French cell phone, all incoming calls are free—so do your best to convince your folks and friends back home to call you.

Bouygues This is smallest of the three French providers.
Ⓦ www.bouygues.fr

Orange Orange is the most widely used provider in France, accounting for nearly half of the country's cell phone users.
Ⓦ www.orange.fr

SFR The second biggest overall provider, SFR claims to have the most extensive network coverage in the country. Ⓦ www.sfr.fr

USING YOUR U.S. CELL PHONE

It may be possible to use your U.S. cell phone during your time in Paris. First, you'll need to make sure that your phone is a "multiband" phone (contact your U.S. service provider for more information). If your phone is indeed multiband, you can sign up for international roaming. International roaming may sound convenient, but be forewarned: It's very expensive and can result in astronomical phone bills. A more affordable option is to switch your phone over to a French calling plan. To do this, you'll need to ask your U.S. service provider to unlock your phone, which allows it to work on other providers' networks.

CALLING HOME

Rest assured, there are several affordable ways to place international calls, so your folks and friends back home won't forget the sound of your voice. But remember: Paris is six hours ahead of the U.S. Atlantic Coast and nine hours ahead of the Pacific, so if you want to catch people at home and awake, you may have to stay up pretty late to do so.

CALLING CARDS

A *carte téléphonique* (calling card) generally provides the best deals on international phone calls. A major advantage of calling cards is that you can use them from any cell phone, phone booth, or landline. A €7.50 or €15 card will give you hundreds or even thousands of minutes for calls abroad. But be sure to shop around. There are a wide variety of calling cards that offer different prices depending on where you're calling and what type of phone you're calling from. To use a French calling card, you first dial an access number, enter a password, and then dial the number of the phone you want to reach, including the country code. You'll find two access numbers on the card: If you choose the local number, you'll get more minutes but you'll have to pay for the local call; if you choose the toll-free number, you'll get fewer minutes but you'll save the cost of the local call. Calling cards typically expire within two months, so be sure to use the minutes you purchase within that time frame. You'll find calling cards for sale at newsstands, tobacco shops, and *epiceries* (small groceries) throughout the city.

DIRECT CALLS

Calling direct is expensive, and long-distance calls from cell phones can be *very* expensive. If you have a contract with a French service provider, you'll be charged anywhere from €1 to €5 per minute, depending on the country you're calling. Costs for calls to the United States depend on the plan you choose. Landlines will offer you better deals than cell phones. France Télécom, the most popular telephone service provider in France, charges about €0.20 per minute and half that during off-peak hours (in general, 7:00 P.M. to 8:00 A.M. during the week and 24 hours on weekends and public holidays). The competing service providers offer package deals for fixed amounts of call time that, in general, work out to be better deals than what France Télécom offers.

Your best bet is to buy a local phone card, which allows you to call long distance via a French number, so you'll only be using up the minutes you've already paid for (see "Calling Cards" for details). You'll most likely also be charged for receiving international calls.

HOW TO DIAL INTERNATIONAL NUMBERS

Here's a quick guide to dialing international numbers from landlines (see the "Country Codes" list in the Appendix for a list of commonly used country codes in Western Europe and North America):

Numbers in the United States Dial 001 + area code + number. For example, dial 001 555 123 4567.

Numbers in other countries Dial 00 + country code + city code + number. To reach someone in Barcelona, Spain, for example, dial 00 34 93 123 4567.

PAYPHONES

You'll find payphones on street corners all over Paris. Unlike in the United States, Parisian payphones do not accept coins. Instead, you'll have to insert either a calling card or your credit card. You can also purchase a *Télécarte,* a special phone card for use in payphones, at post offices, news kiosks, or tobacco shops around town.

VOICE OVER INTERNET PROTOCOL

Voice over Internet Protocol (VoIP) is the most economical choice for making international calls. With it, you place your calls with a computer and a high-speed Internet connection. The cheapest and easiest way to make VoIP calls is to use the computer-to-computer method, which is free if your friends and family have the same equipment you do. Calls to people who do not have VoIP equipment still cots very little—usually less than €0.05/minute for connections to the United States.

To set yourself up to use VoIP, you'll need a headset—or you can use the speakers and microphone that come integrated with most new laptops. If you don't have these items already, a trip to Surcouf (www.surcouf.com) will take care of things. Then, simply download the software from your chosen VoIP provider's website; it's probably best to stick to the big names, such as Vonage and Skype.

- **AIM (an America Online service)** Ⓦ www.aim.com
- **Google Talk** Ⓦ www.google.com/talk
- **Skype** Ⓦ www.skype.com
- **Vonage** Ⓦ www.vonage.com
- **Yahoo** Ⓦ www.yahoo.com

5 THINGS ABOUT THE UNITED STATES YOU WON'T EXPECT TO MISS—BUT WILL

1. **24-hour convenience stores:** "Open All Nite" is pretty much unheard of in France, so try to anticipate those late-night cravings by stocking up on *petits beurres* (cookies) or baguettes.

2. **American television shows in their original language:** *The Simpsons* in French? It's just not natural.

3. **Easy banking:** French banking is not exactly client-friendly. You may be charged for consulting your account on the Internet (maybe €0.50 each time you connect, or a few euros a month for unlimited access), and some banks don't handle cash on certain days of the week.

4. **Mexican food:** Those whose diet in the United States features large quantities of tacos, tamales, and enchiladas will find a gaping hole in Paris, where Mexican cuisine is both hard to come by as well as pricey (not to mention bland and watered-down by American standards).

5. **Sunday, and sometimes Monday, shopping:** While a handful of neighborhoods are lively every day of the week, vast stretches of the city are entirely dead on Sundays, especially in posh residential areas such as the 7th and 16th *arrondissements*. And all over Paris, stores that are open on Saturdays will be closed on Mondays.

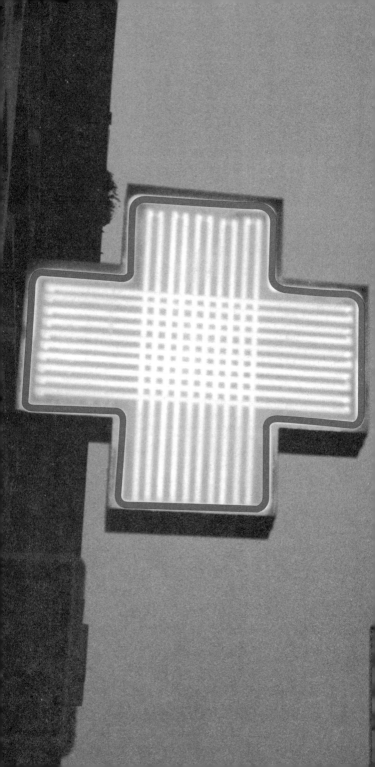

9. Health

You must have adequate health insurance before you leave for Paris. You can't get a student visa without proof of insurance, and of course you'll want to be covered if you get sick or injured. Your school will most likely work with you to make sure you have an appropriate policy for your time in Paris. But if, for whatever reason, your insurance situation is especially complicated, or if you think you may qualify to participate in France's state healthcare system, this chapter offers some quick information that may help.

Rest assured that French doctors are—in all likelihood—just as good as the doctors you're used to back home. Many French doctors who participate in your American insurance plan will be bilingual, so you should be able to easily find an English-speaking doctor if you need one. However, keep in mind that the overwhelming majority of medical encounters, such as visits to the local pharmacy, will be conducted in French. Knowing how to describe your symptoms in French—even if you fumble with the words—will help you get the treatment you need.

HEALTH INSURANCE

Most American insurance plans will reimburse you for your medical expenses, but they won't coordinate billing with European practices. In other words, you'll have to pay for all of your healthcare needs up front and out of pocket. This may sound daunting, but keep in mind that French fees for doctor visits, procedures, and medicines are just a fraction of what they are back home—cost shouldn't stop you from seeking medical attention if you need it.

For French words and phrases pertinent to visits to the doctor, pharmacy, or hospital or in case of medical emergencies, see the Appendix.

Private health insurance plans vary in what they cover. Before leaving for France, verify with your provider exactly what your policy entitles you to and make sure you understand every detail, requirement, and exclusion. Come prepared with your insurance card and claim forms every time you visit a pharmacy, doctor, or hospital. Keep your receipts so that you can get reimbursed. Your insurance company may require detailed forms and receipts translated into English, with euros converted into dollars.

THE FRENCH HEALTHCARE SYSTEM

The French healthcare system, also known as the Centre des Liaisons Européennes et Internationales de Sécurité Sociale (CLEISS), provides some of the highest-quality and most affordable medical care available anywhere. Following are some examples of who is and isn't eligible for French healthcare coverage.

Who is eligible:

- Students under the age of twenty-eight who are registered as full-time students at an affiliated French university

- Anyone who has a contract with a French employer

- E.U. residents

- Anyone who is married or joined by *pacte civil de solidarité* (civil union), or PACS, with a French citizen—you *may* have access through your partner

Who is not eligible:

- Students enrolled in an American study-abroad program

- Students enrolled to study French at a private language-instruction school

- Students *over* the age of twenty-eight who are enrolled in an affiliated French university

- Non-E.U. residents with a long-stay nonstudent visa that does not allow them to work in France

- Tourists

Once affiliated with the French system, you'll receive a *carte vitale,* or insurance card. This card contains all of your personal (but not medical) information and is inscribed with a *numéro INSEE* (Social Security number) that will follow you everywhere you go for as long as you stay in France. When you visit a doctor or pick up prescriptions, your card ensures that up to 70 percent of your medical fees will be reimbursed by the government. To take care of the remaining costs, you have the option of buying a *mutuelle* (complementary health insurance plan), which, although not obligatory, can be advantageous in covering fees incurred by pricier medical procedures and visits to specialists. To complement this coverage, you must either purchase student insurance, which includes options for accident insurance, or show proof of your own American insurance with overseas coverage.

PAYING FOR MEDICAL EXPENSES UNDER FRENCH COVERAGE

Paying for medical expenses is easy if you're covered by the French healthcare system. Once you have a *carte vitale,* the process of being reimbursed following a medical visit is greatly facilitated. More French practitioners are equipped with a machine that will read your card, communicating the visit and its cost to your local *Caisse Primaire d'Assurance Maladie* (CPAM) branch, which then automatically reimburses the money with a direct deposit into your bank account. Otherwise, your doctor will fill out a *feuille de soins* (official health form listing services rendered), which you must sign and send to your CPAM branch in order to be reimbursed. For a visit to a doctor who is *conventionné* (one who charges according to official rates), you'll pay a basic reimbursable fee on the spot. Doctors who are *non-conventionné* may also choose to charge an additional fee, which will not be refunded by insurance.

GETTING HEALTH COVERAGE

If you're in need of health coverage (and you don't qualify for French healthcare), here are a few insurance options:

- **Private French insurance:** You can research private French insurance through companies such as MAAF (www.maaf.fr) or MAE (www.mae.fr), both of which offer special low rates to students and young people.

- **Global medical insurance:** Global medical insurance offers you coverage at home and abroad; find an insurer that offers individual policies.

- **Travel insurance:** Travel insurance policies typically include at least some level of medical and emergency coverage, and many even have specific policies designed for short-term residents of a country. They also provide twenty-four-hour travel assistance and coverage for trip cancellation, interruption, or delay, as well as lost/delayed baggage. Two reliable providers are Travel Guard International (www.travelguard.com) and Travel Insured International (www.travelinsured.com).

PHARMACIES

Unlike in the United States, a pharmacy—rather than your primary care physician—should be your first stop when you're feeling under the weather. Pharmacists can give you an impromptu medical consultation and suggest medication. You may be surprised at the number of ailments they can help you with. French pharmacies are instantly recognizable by the neon green crosses that hang above their entrances; if the cross is lit up, it's open for business. There are twenty-four-hour pharmacies all around town, and you won't be hard pressed to find a good one in your neighborhood. Many pharmacists speak English or are accustomed to interpreting foreigners' best attempts at explaining their symptoms. Here are a few pharmacies in various neighborhoods that cater to English-speakers.

Anglo-American Pharmacy Ⓐ 37 avenue Marceau 75016, Ⓣ 01 47 20 57 37, Ⓜ Alma-Marceau

International Pharmacy of Paris Ⓐ 5 place Pigalle 75017, Ⓣ 01 48 78 38 12, Ⓜ Pigalle

Pharmacie Beaubourg Ⓐ 50 rue Rambuteau 75004, Ⓣ 01 48 87 78 19, Ⓜ Rambuteau

Pharmacie de la Sorbonne Ⓐ 49 rue des Écoles 75005, Ⓣ 01 43 54 26 10, Ⓜ Cluny-La Sorbonne

OVER-THE-COUNTER DRUGS

In Paris, over-the-counter drugs are kept behind the counter. This means that you'll have to speak with a pharmacist for all of your medication needs, however minor or embarrassing. There's little difference between France and the United States when it comes to what drugs are sold without prescriptions. If you have a run-of-the-mill headache, cold, flu, or upset stomach, you'll likely be able to get the medicine you need without a prescription. If you're not sure what you need or don't know the French equivalent of a particular American drug, describe your symptoms and ask the pharmacist for help. Remember that pharmacists know drugs by their generic names, as brand names differ by country. If you are looking for the French equivalent of a particular American drug, bring your old bottle or package with you to show the pharmacists.

TYPES OF PHARMACIES

In addition to traditional *pharmacies,* you'll find pharmacies in Paris that are devoted to homeopathic medicine and products as well as *herboristes,* which provide treatments and remedies derived from medicinal plants and essential oils. And while pharmacies will take care of all your medicine needs, *parapharmacies* provide a larger selection of toiletries and beauty products, but no drugs.

PRESCRIPTION DRUGS

To obtain prescription drugs in France, you must present at any pharmacy a valid *ordonnance* (prescription) from a French doctor. You'll pay full price for all prescriptions, but remember that prescription drugs in France are substantially less expensive than they are in the United States. Be sure to verify what type of prescription-drug coverage your American insurance provides, as well as what the claim procedures involve. If you're covered by the French system, when you present your *carte vitale* you'll pay only the percentage of the drug's cost that is not taken care of by basic insurance. If you have a *mutuelle* (complementary insurance), part or all of this remaining fee will also be covered for you.

Be aware that if you're eligible for French coverage, after you apply, your card could take a very long time to arrive. If you haven't received it yet, you'll have to pay up front for your prescriptions, but you can ask the pharmacist to provide you with a *feuille de soins* to mail to your CPAM branch so you can be reimbursed.

VISITING THE DOCTOR

Fortunately, you'll have no problem finding an English-speaking doctor, dentist, or mental health professional in Paris. For comprehensive listings of English-speaking health professionals, visit the U.S. Embassy's website at http://france.usembassy.gov. For any appointment, be sure to first check with your insurance provider about the coverage you're entitled to and whom you're permitted to see. Here's an overview of the different types of doctors you might see during your stay, as well as some advice on what to expect from your visits.

- **Physicians:** Like in the United States, doctors may be either generalists or specialists. If you have French healthcare coverage, you'll first have to choose a generalist and declare this to your CPAM office. To see a specialist, you'll first have to visit your generalist and attain a referral so that you can be reimbursed. A specialist's referral, however, is by no means obligatory if you want to see a generalist.

- **Dentists:** Dental facilities may be less blindingly bright and sterile-seeming than those in the United States, but rest assured that the quality of care is up to par. Dental procedures such as cleanings and fillings are substantially cheaper in France than they are back home. Depending on your insurance situation, you'll be either partially or wholly reimbursed for whatever work you have done.

- **Ophthalmologists:** Don't expect to benefit from drastic savings if you plan to buy new eyeglasses during your time in France. If you have French healthcare, you won't be reimbursed for frames, but you may be partially reimbursed for lenses if you submit a written attestation from your ophthalmologist stating that your prescription needs to be changed. Ophthalmologist visits are covered by the French system, but visits to the optometrist are not, as the latter is not recognized as an official medical practitioner in France.

- **Mental health professionals:** English-speaking psychotherapists and social workers can help you with whatever issues you may be facing. French healthcare does not provide coverage for consultations with mental health professionals, so you'll have to be prepared to pay out of pocket.

- **Gynecologists:** Leave your modesty at home, because you won't get to wear a paper gown during your visit to the gynecologist. Instead, you'll most likely be asked to disrobe entirely. In general, the French manner of conducting medical visits is more straightforward and unembarrassed than in the United States.

HOSPITALS/EMERGENCY ROOMS

The French hospital system comes in two variations: public and private. Public hospitals provide excellent care for negligible cost if you're covered by insurance, French or otherwise. Private hospitals are not necessarily of higher quality, and you may not be reimbursed by your health insurance plan for the room cost and doctor's fee. However, one reason to seek out private treatment would be if you wanted to ensure English service at the American Hospital, located to the west of Paris. For other hospitals where English is spoken, visit the U.S. Embassy's website. For information on whom to call in the event of a medical emergency or if you're in need of an ambulance, see Chapter 18, "Emergencies." At the following locations, emergency care is provided 24/7, which is not the case at all Parisian hospitals.

American Hospital of Paris Ⓐ 63 boulevard Victor Hugo 92200 Neuilly-sur-Seine, Ⓣ 01 46 41 25 01, Ⓜ Pont de Levallois

l Hôtel Dieu Ⓐ 1 place du Parvis Notre-Dame 75004, Ⓣ 01 42 34 82 34, Ⓜ Cité

Hôpital Pitié-Salpetrière Ⓐ 47–83 boulevard de l'Hôpital 75013, Ⓣ 01 42 16 00 00, Ⓜ St-Marcel

Hôpital St-Louis Ⓐ 1 avenue Claude Vellefaux 75010, Ⓣ 01 42 49 49 49, Ⓜ Goncourt

9. HEALTH

WOMEN'S HEALTH LEXICON

Here are a few terms pertinent to women's health that you may need to know if you consult a gynecologist or pharmacist:

avortement/IVG	abortion
cystite	urinary tract infection
douleurs des règles	menstrual cramps
frottis	Pap smear
kyste	cyst
maladies sexuellement transmissibles	sexually transmitted diseases
mycose vaginale	yeast infection
pilule	birth-control pill
pilule du lendemain	morning-after pill
(avoir tes) règles	(to have your) period
saignements	bleeding
teste de grossesse	pregnancy test

SEXUAL HEALTH

Obtaining birth-control pills in Paris is relatively easy and inexpensive (usually under €20 for a three-month supply). You'll just need to first get a prescription from a French gynecologist. Or consider getting your American doctor to prescribe a six-month or a one-year supply of birth-control pills and fill the prescription all at once (if your insurance won't allow that, you can refill the prescription from Paris and have the monthly packets sent to you). The morning-after pill is also available from pharmacies in Paris, no prescription needed. It must be taken within seventy-two hours following unprotected sex to be effective.

In France, abortion is legal through the end of the twelfth week of pregnancy. To get an abortion, you'll be required to schedule two medical consultations, separated by a one-week period of reflection. Minors need no parental consent to undergo an abortion, but they must be accompanied by someone over the age of eighteen. The procedure is performed in any number of hospitals and private clinics in Paris and generally costs between €200 and €300. If you have French healthcare, 80 percent of the procedure can be covered. Visit the French family planning website for further details (www.planning-familial.org).

SEXUAL HEALTH CLINICS

The following are a few clinics that offer free, anonymous testing for HIV and other sexually transmitted diseases. The abbreviation CDAG stands for *Centre de Dépistage Anonyme et Gratuit,* or anonymous free testing center.

- **CDAG Belleville** Ⓐ 218 rue de Belleville 75020, Ⓣ 01 40 33 52 00, Ⓜ Télégraphe
- **CDAG Figuier** Ⓐ 2 rue du Figuier 75004, Ⓣ 01 49 96 62 70, Ⓜ Pont-Marie, St-Paul
- **CDAG Ridder** Ⓐ 3 rue de Ridder 75014, Ⓣ 01 58 14 30 30, Ⓜ Plaisance

5 IDEAS FOR CONQUERING HOMESICKNESS

1. **Bagels:** Head to the Jewish heart of the Marais for a taste of New York in the form of a delicious bagel from the Eastern European–style bakery and café Korcarz. Ⓐ 29 rue des Rosiers 75004, Ⓣ 01 42 77 39 47, Ⓜ St-Paul

2. **Greasy spoons:** Get your bottomless cup of coffee and eggs any style at the diner-style restaurant Breakfast in America. Ⓐ 17 rue des Écoles 75005, Ⓣ 01 43 54 50 28, Ⓜ Cardinal-Lemoine

3. **American movies:** You'll have no problem finding Hollywood blockbusters in English in Paris, especially at chains such as MK2 (Ⓦ http://mk2.fr), UGC (Ⓦ www.ugc.fr), and Gaumont (Ⓦ www.cinemasgaumontpathe.com).

4. **American groceries:** Stroll through aisles stocked with Jif peanut butter, Aunt Jemima pancake mix, and other American products at American-foods grocery store Thanksgiving. Ⓐ 20 rue St-Paul 75004, Ⓣ 01 42 77 68 28, Ⓜ St-Paul

5. **Chinese food:** There's something so familiar and dependable about Chinese restaurants. Paris has several Chinese neighborhoods, the biggest and most well-known in the 13th *arrondissement*. One great restaurant choice is Li Ka Fo. Ⓐ 39 avenue de Choisy 75013, Ⓣ 01 45 84 20 45, Ⓜ Porte de Choisy

10. Getting Involved

Moving beyond your student horizons can take some effort. While your schoolwork will probably be your first priority, make the most of your time by getting involved in life outside of school (schedule permitting, of course). You'll find endless opportunities to do so in Paris, whether you're conducting scientific research through an internship, serving espresso at a café, or volunteering at a neighborhood hospital.

French university students often already know each other well, keeping friendships they formed in childhood. They tend to pursue their higher education close to home, and—in contrast with American students—many have no qualms about living with their parents while they're in college. To foreign students studying in Paris, they can appear to be awfully cliquey. Just remember that, in general, friendships take more time and perseverance to develop here.

MEETING LOCALS

It sounds like a study abroad cliché, but making an effort to befriend Parisians should be a requirement during your time in Paris. Locals are excellent sources of practical and personal insight into the city, and the relationships you develop with them, whether it be the neighborhood newspaper vendor, the owner of the corner bar, or the chain-smoking guy in your French literature class, will give you knowledge that would be impossible to gain hanging out with just Americans.

WHERE TO MEET PARISIANS

Your university is an obvious place to start your pursuit of Parisian friendships, whether you're lingering in the halls during breaks between classes or getting involved in extracurricular activities or classes. Here are some ideas, both within and outside of school:

- Join an intramural sports team or participate in a sports club (see Chapter 13, "Sports")

- Volunteer (see "Volunteer Opportunities" later in this chapter)

- Join one of the student syndicates that are so popular at Paris universities and get involved in student activism

- Go to a bar or club on a designated intercultural night

- Sign up for a language class through your local *mairie,* or town hall

CONVERSATION EXCHANGES

If you want to meet a new Parisian friend and bone up on your French language skills at the same time, consider answering or posting an ad for an *échange linguistique* (conversation exchange). During a conversation exchange, you and a native French speaker meet for an hour or so, talking half the time in French and the other half in English. You can find and post ads on bulletin boards at your university (especially in languages departments) and in municipal libraries. Or try the "Strictly Conversation" section of FUSAC magazine (www.fusac.fr).

DATING

Though Paris is, presumably, the city of romance, most people find romance in the same ways they find it in other cities: through friends, at school, at work, in bars, and by chance. You should know that relationship and sexual mores in France are more liberal than in the United States. For instance, dating more than one person at a time is not at all considered taboo. Here are a few tips for navigating the dating scene in Paris:

- **Unwanted advances:** Despite the politeness that predominates, French men can be decidedly more brazen than American men—though they'll generally back down once you've failed to show interest.

- **Asking out:** It's not at all unusual for women to do the asking out. If a man does it, he'll generally insist on paying. Women, however, aren't usually expected to pay, even when they do the asking out (in this case, splitting the bill may be the best solution).

- **Showing interest:** If you take the initiative of calling someone to see about making plans, this will be interpreted as a definite sign of interest. The French are just not known to be forward about making friendships.

- **First dates:** Not unlike in the United States, it's more common to spend a first date over a meal or a drink in public than in one's apartment. Movies aren't especially common first dates, nor are group situations like parties.

ONLINE DATING

Internet dating sites aren't as popular in Paris as they are in the United States, but they are gaining traction. Both www.softdating.com and www.netinthecity.com offer listings of upcoming speed-dating events in Paris. And www.expatica.com and www.meetic.com are popular choices for online dating.

CLUBS, ORGANIZATIONS, AND OTHER RESOURCES

Paris has an enormous international student community and an astonishing array of social organizations, including several groups that connect American and other foreign students. Before you leave, you can check out groups' websites to access online message boards and newsletters—all of which can give you insight on living in Paris. Look for groups that provide services or events that match your interests, and be sure to check with your university about student groups.

EXPAT RESOURCES

Social groups are a great place to rub shoulders with other Americans, and there are also a number of bars, bookstores, and other places that draw an American crowd. (For a list of English-language bookstores, see Chapter 7, "Studying & Staying Informed"). There's also a wide selection of expat resources that provide advice on everything from finding housing to finding new friends. You can start your investigation here.

Easy Expat This website offers information on finding apartments, school and volunteer opportunities, overseas jobs, and healthcare. Ⓦ www.easyexpat.com

France-États-Unis This club promotes cross-cultural exchange, organizing get-togethers over drinks or dinner, for various cultural events, and to attend speeches. Ⓦ www.france-etatsunis.com

Living Abroad This network for travelers, students, and expats offers a forum for sharing advice about and resources for the cross-cultural experience. Ⓦ www.liveabroad.coM

Meetup This popular site gives international travelers a place to meet others with similar interests, swap travel experiences, and establish communities abroad. Ⓦ www.meetup.com

Paris Alumnae/i Network For college graduates, this group connects graduates of anglophone universities worldwide for social, cultural, and educational activities and networking opportunities. Ⓦ www.pan-paris.org

STUDENT ORGANIZATIONS

To find out about all the student groups available to you in Paris, contact Anima'Fac, Paris's network of student associations (08 20 36 07 32, www.animafac.net). Here are a few student groups worth exploring.

Cité Internationale Universitaire There's always something going on at this residential campus, where students from all over the world live in nearly forty different international houses. Even if you don't live here, you can attend a number of conferences, concerts, exhibitions, and more. Ⓐ 17 boulevard Jourdan 75014, Ⓣ 01 44 16 64 00, Ⓦ www.ciup.fr, Ⓜ Cité Universitaire

Le Club International des Jeunes à Paris (CIJP) CIJP offers regular activities, such as language exchanges and trips, to help you meet other students studying in Paris. Joining CIJP is a great way to meet students beyond those in your classes. Ⓣ 01 43 06 23 16, Ⓦ www.club-international.org

Communauté d'Entraide et Réseau d'Information et de Soutien des Étudiants Internationaux en France (CERISE) This group, whose name means "Information and Support Network of the International Students in France," helps international students to settle into their new lives in Paris. Ⓦ www.bienvenueenfrance.net

Erasmus Erasmus is the Europe-wide university exchange program, and its participants are all over Paris. While Americans can't participate in Erasmus, any young, international type can infiltrate its activities. *Soirées Erasmus* are notoriously rowdy affairs and are often advertised on university bulletin boards. Ⓦ www.ec.europa.edu

Euro-Fil This citywide group connects students from all over the world. The group has weekly meetings and is an excellent way to meet other students who are struggling to settle in. It's a great resource for both fun events and practical information. Ⓣ 06 85 62 03 17, Ⓦ www.eurofil.fr.st

VOLUNTEER OPPORTUNITIES

Paris offers endless opportunities to get involved in volunteer work—even if you have only one free afternoon each week, and even if your French isn't up to par. Serving meals at a homeless shelter, tutoring, and visiting patients in a hospital are just some of the possibilities. Be sure to check out what opportunities are available through your school, and visit the website www.espacebenevolat.org, a volunteerism portal. Here are a few other places to contact.

Action Contre la Faim This organization combats malnutrition and famine in developing countries worldwide. Ⓐ 4 rue Niepce 75014, Ⓣ 01 43 35 88 88, Ⓦ www.aidez.org, Ⓜ Pernety

Armée du Salut The French branch of the Salvation Army delivers meals to homeless people and runs shelters, day centers, and retirement and maternity homes, among its many other missions. Ⓐ 60 rue des Frères Flavien 75020, Ⓣ 01 43 62 25 60, Ⓦ www.armeedusalut.fr, Ⓜ Porte des Lilas

Croix-Rouge The French branch of the Red Cross has a mission of social action and education. Opportunities are always changing. See its website for details. Ⓐ 12 rue Chardin 75016, Ⓣ 01 44 14 69 23, Ⓦ http://paris08.croix-rouge.fr, Ⓜ Passy

Restos du Cœur This well-known organization sets up soup stands around the city, hands out food and supplies to needy families, and runs a shelter on a boat near the Bibliothèque Nationale. Ⓐ 4 cité d'Hauteville 75010, Ⓣ 01 53 24 98 00, Ⓦ www.frequenceevasion.com/restosducoeur.htm, Ⓜ Poissonière

Visites des Malades dans les Établissements Hospitaliers This association seeks volunteers to visit hospitals and retirement homes to provide companionship for ill and elderly patients. Ⓐ 8 bis avenue René Coty 75014, Ⓣ 01 43 20 87 97, Ⓦ www.vmeh-national.com, Ⓜ Denfert-Rochereau

LGBT ORGANIZATIONS

Paris has a very open and visible gay community, and there are a wide variety of gay and lesbian groups—social, political, and professional—worth checking out. *Têtu* (www.tetu.com), a popular magazine for the gay community, is a good place to start your search. Another great resource is the Centre Gai Lesbien Paris-Île de France, a social center for the LGBT community that hosts many organizations. Extensive information is available on the website.

Centre gai lesbien Paris-Île de France Ⓐ 3 rue Keller 75011, Ⓣ 01 43 57 21 47, Ⓦ http://cglparis. org, Ⓜ Ledru-Rollin or Voltaire

5 CHEAP DATES, PARIS-STYLE

1. **Get a bird's eye view:** Head to the roof of the Institut du Monde Arabe (the Arab Institute), a cool building whose exterior is covered with lenses that open and close according to the amount of sunlight. Ⓦ www.imarabe.org, Ⓜ Sully-Morland

2. **Take a graveyard stroll:** Pay your respects to legendary twelfth-century lovers Abélard and Héloïse by visiting their side-by-side graves in the Père-Lachaise cemetery. An early evening stroll (the cemetery is open until 6:00 P.M.) can be both spooky and romantic. Ⓜ Philippe-Auguste, Gambetta, or Père-Lachaise.

3. **See the lights:** Parisian monuments are lit up to sublime effect when the sun goes down. Check out the Cour Carrée, the area in front of and near the Louvre. The glowing pyramid that covers the Louvre's entrance is one of Paris's most romantic sights. Ⓜ Palais Royal-Musée du Louvre

4. **Enjoy a free meal:** Many neighborhood café-bars around town offer complimentary couscous meals on Friday and Saturday nights. Ask around to find the locals' favorites, and head out for a super-cheap date.

5. **Walk the banks of the Seine:** Few things are more romantic, or more Parisian, than a stroll along the Seine. The stretch around Île St-Louis is particularly lovely. Ⓜ Pont-Marie, Sully-Morland

BONJOUR
GOOD MORNING

11. Working

B efore you get too excited about the idea of working during your time abroad, talk to an adviser in your study-abroad office to learn more about what you're in for. On the one hand, working means more money to enjoy Paris—after all, Paris is one of the world's most expensive cities. It also presents a unique opportunity to get to know French culture up close and personal.

However, working also means facing a time-consuming job search, along with a visa application process so convoluted that it will leave your head spinning. And when you do finally start working, the time you spend tending bar or tutoring means less time to study, travel, bar-hop, see museums, and do all the other cool activities that brought you to Paris in the first place.

JOB HUNTING

Here are some quick tips for finding work in Paris. If you're looking for food service–type jobs, focus on trendier and more touristy areas of the city as well as gathering places for anglophone and international crowds. There are loads of such places in Paris—the Bastille and the Marais are good neighborhoods to start with.

- **Newspapers:** You'll find extensive help wanted sections in newspapers such as *Libération, Le Monde,* and *Le Figaro,* and their online versions (www. liberation.fr, www.lemond.fr, and www.lefigaro.fr).

- **Websites:** There are job listings on websites such as France's Monster site, www. monster.fr, and the website of the national employment agency, www. anpe.fr. Check out anglophone-focused listings on the Craigslist Paris website (http://paris.craigs list.org) and in *FUSAC* magazine (www.fusac.fr).

- **Student resources:** Two student/youth associations post open positions: the CROUS de Paris (www.crous-paris.fr) and Le Centre d'Information et de Documentation Jeunesse (www.cidj.fr).

- **Networking:** As with most job searches, networking will probably be your most effective tool. A good place to start is by finding out whether your home university has an alumnae organization in Paris. Another good resource for job postings are bulletin boards at the American Church (www.acparis.org).

TYPES OF JOBS

Your native language already makes you eminently qualified for several jobs, including teaching English, tutoring, child care, and café and restaurant work (especially in anglophone establishments). Of course, this being Paris, the vast majority of opportunities will require adequate French as well. Many part-time jobs will pay the minimum wage, or SMIC (*salaire minimum interprofessionnel de croissance*), which is currently just over €8 an hour.

INTERNSHIPS

More and more students are incorporating internships into their time abroad—either during the semester or during the summer after classes end. An internship can be an excellent opportunity to explore a possible career path or have an extra experience during your time abroad. Your university's study-abroad office is your best resource for learning more.

The following websites also offer general information on overseas internships.

- **Center for Cultural Interchange** Ⓦ www.cci-exchange.com
- **Global Experiences** Ⓦ www.globalexperiences.com/internships
- **Global Youth Opportunity** Ⓦ www.globalyouthopportunity.com
- **Institute for the International Education of Students** Ⓦ www.iesabroad.org
- **Intern Abroad** Ⓦ www.internabroad.com
- **Internships in Francophone Europe** Ⓦ www.ifeparis.org
- **International Internships** Ⓦ www.internationalinternships.com
- **Transitions Abroad** Ⓦ www.transitionsabroad.com/listings/work/internships/index.shtml

WORKING UNDER THE TABLE

Many young people from abroad engage in under-the-table work during their time in France, taking on such undocumented jobs as working in a bar or café run by a willing owner. Though these are popular options, this kind of work setup is illegal for both employee and employer. Even if the chances of being caught are slim, know that you're taking a risk if you choose this route.

TEACHING ENGLISH

Teaching English is among the most in-demand occupations for young Americans living in Paris. The pay is typically mediocre, but the work is rewarding—and the experience gives a boost to your résumé. There are numerous options, depending on your preferences for the age and level of the students with whom you wish to work:

- **Paris public schools:** If you're interested in teaching elementary, middle, or high school students in Paris public schools, apply to the Rectorat de Paris (www.ac-paris.fr), the administrative institution that runs the school system. Send your résumé and cover letter anytime, as teachers sometimes leave without warning and need to be replaced mid-year. This is a great job if you're a student, because you will be granted a work permit almost immediately (the perks of working for the state) and can often negotiate your schedule with the school. The commitment may be anywhere from six to sixteen hours a week, and hours are sometimes divided between schools.

- **Private schools:** Paris has a number of private schools that specialize in teaching English to adults, typically businesspeople. For example, you'll see ads all over the Métro for the Wall Street Institute ("I speak English—Wall Street English!"). See the website for more details (www.wallstreetinstitute.fr). Other private language schools to check out include Inlingua (www.inlingua-paris.com) and Oise Intensive Language Schools (www.oise.com).

- **Université de Paris:** Young people sometimes find work as language assistants at one of the thirteen branches of the University of Paris in and around the city. These schools may already have exchange programs with specific American, British, or Australian universities, which means that most English-teaching positions will be filled, but you can try to gain employment via *candidature spontanée* (unsolicited application) by sending in your résumé and cover letter. Apply for this kind of job in the springtime for the following year, as decisions are made relatively early, and you'll have to be in the United States to pick up your visa.

Teaching English as a Foreign Language (TEFL) courses provide lesson plans, teaching practice, and assistance in finding overseas teaching jobs. While enrolling in one of these monthlong courses can't hurt, keep in mind that many employers are just looking for native English-speaking teachers and couldn't care less about their certifications. Two of the most reputable TEFL courses are the Cambridge Certificate in English Language Teaching to Adults (www.cambridgeesol.org) and the Trinity Certificate in Teaching English to Speakers of Other Languages (www.trinitycollege.co.uk). The programs can be expensive—most cost around $2,000. For more information and a full list of courses, check out www.tefl.com.

TUTORING

Tutoring is among the easiest jobs to come by in Paris. To find tutoring jobs, post fliers advertising your skills at universities, libraries, bookstores, and other places frequented by people interested in learning languages. One of the great things about this option is that you can fix your own rates: Tutors generally ask for €15–€20 per hour. This sort of work is always "off the books" because it's just two people negotiating an exchange of services. As a safety precaution, be sure to meet in a public place.

Another option is to apply to an online tutoring company, such as Keep School (www.keepschool.com). For your services, you'll be paid twice a month directly to your bank account according to fixed rates—but this means you'll have to open a French bank account to be paid. Schools that specialize in teaching English to businesspeople often seek private tutors as well.

AU PAIR WORK

Any unmarried high school graduate between the ages of eighteen and thirty can spend up to eighteen months in France working as an au pair. As a live-in babysitter, you will stay with a French family and care for the children in addition to performing certain duties around the house. You'll be expected to work about five hours a day, thirty hours a week, while attending obligatory French classes. In exchange, you'll receive a private room, three meals a day, and Social Security coverage, as well as a monthly allowance that will take care of the cost of your transportation pass and class tuition.

You must apply to work as an au pair while still in the United States, a process that will take up to four months. Start by contacting an au pair agency in Paris to get the initial applications forms. The website of the Union Française des Associations Au Pair, www.ufaap.org, is a good source of information and names of au pair agencies. The agency will then assign you to a family and apply for a contract on your behalf from the state agency for foreign workers. Once you have your contract, you can go to your local French Consulate to apply for an au pair visa. Verify what documents are required on your consulate's website before going to apply in person.

BABYSITTING

Babysitting jobs are relatively easy to come by in Paris. Speaking with French children is a great way to practice your French—they'll let you know right away when you make mistakes. You'll find plenty of ads in newspapers and on community bulletin boards seeking English-speaking babysitters. Wednesdays are especially in demand, because French schoolchildren have the day off; late afternoons, when school lets out, are other good times. The weekly commitment is generally not huge, and you can expect to be paid around minimum wage.

GETTING PAPERWORK IN ORDER

The primary obstacle to working in France is getting legal permission to do so. Work visas, which are granted by the French government and required for aboveboard jobs, are not easy to come by. As a student visa holder, you're theoretically entitled to work up to nineteen and a half hours per week during the year (and thirty-nine hours per week during vacations), but the student visa itself won't suffice as a work permit. Before you may work, you must first receive a job offer from a French employer—then apply to the French Labor Ministry for the actual authorization. This work permit is valid for three months and can be renewed if you continue studying in France.

French Ministry of Labor Ⓐ 123 boulevard de la Villette 75010, Ⓣ 01 44 84 42 86, Ⓦ www.travail.gouv.fr, Ⓜ Jaurés, Stalingrad

5 THINGS THAT WILL MAKE YOUR FRIENDS BACK HOME JEALOUS

1. **French baking:** Any morning you feel so inclined, you can get a warm *pain au chocolat* (chocolate croissant) from your local bakery. And warm *baguettes* . . . and we won't even mention those French pastries. . .

2. **French architecture:** You'll never tire of exploring Paris's super-charming apartment buildings, and living in an amazing sixteenth-century building will make you feel connected to history in a way you probably haven't experienced back home.

3. **French wine:** €3 will buy you a perfectly decent bottle of wine, whether it's a *burgundy, merlot, chablis, côtes du rhone*, or . . .

4. **French food:** Any trip to the dairy section of the supermarket, with its mouth-watering selection of cheeses from *camembert* to *morbier* to *Roquefort,* will remind you how lucky you are to be in a country so renowned for its incredible cuisine.

5. **French *esprit*:** While Starbucks storefronts are steadily popping up, the independent spirit still reigns supreme in Paris, where one-of-a-kind cafés and book and record stores are not the endangered species they seem to be in other big cities.

12. Fitness & Beauty

The French ability to maintain a svelte physique despite a notoriously rich diet is mind-boggling—and it's certainly not due to the fact that France is a nation of fitness freaks. Regular workouts aren't really integrated into people's schedules the way they are for many health-conscious Americans. However, if you're looking for more ways to get yourself moving, plenty of options are available in Paris, whether you prefer weight-lifting or a walk in the park. Paris has many health clubs, but the spaces themselves may offer fewer facilities than what you're used to back home. If you prefer to exercise outdoors, the city's numerous parks are perfect for a power walk or a run.

When it comes to beauty, Paris is famous for its luxe shops and salons; but many of these will, sadly, be out of a student's budget. However, you'll find plenty of affordable places to get your hair cut or styled and, if you're in the mood to treat yourself, plenty of relaxing, indulgent spas and Turkish steam baths.

GYMS AND SPORTS CLUBS

The best way to get your gym time in is at your school, where exercise facilities are generally available for free or a minimal fee. Twenty-four-hour gyms are pretty much unheard of in France, and opening hours tend to be more limited than what you're probably used to in the United States. However, classes and facilities are generally comparable. If swimming is your exercise of choice, know that even high-end gyms may not have pools, so be sure to research the options thoroughly. On the low end, gyms will run you about €500 for a yearlong membership of €200 for a trimester.

Club Jean de Beauvais Ⓐ 5 rue Jean de Beauvais 75005, Ⓣ 01 46 33 16 80, www.spajeandebeauvais.fr, Ⓜ Maubert-Mutualité

Club Med Gym Ⓐ 10 place de la République 75010, Ⓣ 01 47 00 69 98, Ⓦ www.clubmedgym.com, Ⓜ République

Club Quartier Latin Ⓐ 19 rue de Pontoise 75005, Ⓣ 01 55 42 77 88, Ⓦ www.clubquartierlatin.com, Ⓜ Cardinal Lemoine

Sun City Sport Ⓐ 90 avenue de St-Ouen 75018, Ⓣ 01 42 29 16 83, Ⓦ www.suncity-sport.com, Ⓜ Guy Môquet

Vit'Halles Beaubourg Ⓐ 48 rue Rambuteau 75003, Ⓣ 01 42 77 21 71, Ⓦ www.vithalles.com, Ⓜ Rambuteau

SWIMMING POOLS

There are about thirty-five municipal swimming pools in Paris, so you're never too far from a swim, rain or shine (most pools are indoors). Prices are reasonable, usually less than €3 and less than €2 if you're under twenty-six, and you can choose to pay each time you go, get a card that allows you ten entries, or buy a three-month pass that allows you unlimited access. Be sure to wear a swimming cap, as well as a Speedo-style suit if you're male—both are requirements at municipal swimming pools. For a complete list of Paris's municipal swimming pools, go to www.paris.fr. Here are a few popular choices.

Piscine Butte aux Cailles Ⓐ 5 place Paul Verlaine 75013, Ⓣ 01 45 89 60 05, Ⓜ Corvisart

Piscine Cours des Lions Ⓐ 115–119 boulevard de Charonne, 75011, Ⓣ 01 44 93 28 18, Ⓜ Alexandre Dumas

Piscine St-Germain Ⓐ 12 rue Lobineau 75006, Ⓣ 01 56 81 25 40, Ⓜ Mabillon

Piscine St-Merri Ⓐ 16 rue du Renard 75004, Ⓣ 01 42 72 29 45, Ⓜ Rambuteau

Piscine Suzanne Berlioux Ⓐ 10 place de la Rotonde, Forum des Halles niveau -3 75001 Ⓣ 01 42 36 98 44, Ⓜ Les Halles

RUNNING

Few people jog on the sidewalks in Paris due to the excessive human and automobile traffic. Parks provide a much better option for your daily run, even if you have to take the Métro or brave a few blocks of pavement before leaving urban obstacles in the dust. If you're looking for group running, the Mairie de Paris organizes free Sunday morning jogs in many of the city's public parks. These start at 9 A.M. and are led by trained professionals. Check out the website of the Mairie de Paris for details.

Bois de Vincennes Located east of Paris, the Bois de Vincennes is the largest green space in the city, well-insulated from noise and pollution. It offers dozens of different paths for running. Ⓜ Porte de Charenton, Porte Dorée

Bois de Boulogne The city's other enormous park, the Bois de Boulogne, is located just west of Paris and is home to the Longchamp horse races and French Open tennis tournament. The running paths here are plentiful and peaceful. Ⓜ Porte Maillot

Jardin du Luxembourg and Jardin des Tuileries In the Jardin du Luxembourg, you'll do your miles on the same gravel paths where Hemingway used to run. In the Jardin des Tuileries, you'll be surrounded by some of Paris's most famous sites, including the Louvre to the east and the Seine to the south. Ⓜ Tuileries for Jardin du Luxembourg, Concorde for Jardin des Tuileries

Parc des Buttes Chaumont Located in the 19th *arrondisse-ment,* the Parc des Buttes Chaumont is one of Paris's largest and loveliest parks, with gentle hills, waterfalls, and fantastic panoramic views of the city. It's a great place to struggle through some hill work, and there are both paved and dirt paths. Ⓜ Buttes-Chaumont, Botzaris

Parc des Mais It would be hard to name a more postcard-perfect running spot than this park in front of the Eiffel Tower. Ⓜ Champ de Mars-Tour Eiffel, École Militaire

YOGA AND PILATES

Aficionados will be happy to know that both yoga and Pilates have been embraced by the French. Private and group classes for all levels and many different techniques are offered in hundreds of locations, including some sports clubs (inquire at individual clubs for details), where classes may come as part of your membership. Here are some well-known venues.

Centre Sivananda de Yoga Vedanta de Paris Ten yoga classes cost €99 for adults, €89 for students. Ⓐ 123 boulevard de Sébastopol 75002, Ⓣ 01 40 26 77 49, Ⓦ www.sivananda. org/paris, Ⓜ Strasbourg-St-Denis

Centre de Yoga du Marais Five yoga classes cost €70; ten classes cost €125. Ⓐ 72 rue du Vertbois 75003, Ⓣ 01 42 74 24 92, Ⓦ www.yogamarais.com, Ⓜ Temple

Core Body Centre Pilates A single-mat class or one-hour yoga class costs €25. Ⓐ 76 bis rue des St-Pères 75006, Ⓣ 01 45 49 97 29, Ⓦ www.corebodypilates.com, Ⓜ Sèvres-Babylone

Le Studio Pilates de Paris A single-class costs €28. Ⓐ 39 rue du Temple 75003, Ⓣ 01 42 72 91 74, Ⓦ www. studiopilatesdeparis.com, Ⓜ Hôtel de Ville

Paris Yoga A single yoga or Pilates class costs €18; a five-class voucher valid for two months costs €80 for adults and €75 for students. Ⓐ 9 rue Magellan 75008, Ⓣ 01 40 70 14 44, Ⓦ www.parisyoga.com, Ⓜ Georges V

HAIR SALONS/BARBERS

In general, a budget haircut in Paris is €20–€30, and a more upscale one could cost €80–€100 or more. The salons listed here are hair salons only, without nail or waxing services.

Aveda Salon (English-speaking) Ⓐ 55 rue de Bellechasse 75007, Ⓣ 01 45 55 85 69, Ⓜ Solférino

Coiffure 27 (budget) Ⓐ 27 rue Oberkampf 75011, Ⓣ 01 43 55 07 47, Ⓜ Oberkampf

Roman Kramer Salon (English-speaking) Ⓐ 13 bis rue des Plantes 75014, Ⓣ 01 40 44 61 34, Ⓜ Mouton Duernet

Toni & Guy Ⓐ 248 rue St-Honoré 75001, Ⓣ 01 40 20 98 20, Ⓜ Palais Royal-Musée du Louvre

Ultra Ⓐ 3 rue St-Sabin 75011, Ⓣ 01 43 57 42 67, Ⓜ Bastille

SPAS

If you want a bit of pampering or to escape the chilly dampness of a Parisian winter, you'll have your choice of spas—though you'll pay an arm and a leg for the pampering privilege: A massage can cost €80 or more. Paris offers luxurious modern spas as well as traditional, old-world style *hammams* (Turkish baths) where you can go to sink into a drowsy delirium for hours at a time.

Hammam de la Mosquée de Paris Offers a steam bath and massages; admission to the *hammam* is €15, and massages cost extra. Ⓐ 2 bis place du Puits de l'Ermite 75005, Ⓣ 01 45 35 97 33, Ⓦ www.mosquee-de-paris.net, Ⓜ Place Monge

La Bulle Kenzo Offers a range of high-end services in a chic, trendy environment. Expect to pay a lot here—like €80 for a massage. Ⓐ 1 rue du Pont Neuf 75001, Ⓣ 01 73 04 20 04, Ⓦ www.labullekenzo.com, Ⓜ Pont Neuf

Spa Nuxe, Printemps de la Beauté A luxurious spa inside the Printemps department store with a range of services, including massage. Ⓐ Printemps Haussmann Beauté Maison 1ère étage, 64 boulevard Haussmann 75009, Ⓣ 01 42 82 52 52, Ⓦ http://departmentstoreparis.printemps.com, Ⓜ Havre-Caumartin

5 CHEAP, TOURISTY THINGS YOU'VE GOT TO DO

1. **The Rodin Museum:** Visit its beautiful rose gardens to see more of the beloved sculptor's works. Admission: €1. Ⓐ 79 rue de Varenne 75007, Ⓣ 01 44 18 61 10, Ⓦ www.musee-rodin.fr, Ⓜ Invalides

2. **The Panthéon:** Soak in the genius of famous figures like Voltaire, Rousseau, Marie Curie, and many others at this imposing mausoleum for approximately eighty of France's greatest minds. Admission: €7.50 adults, €4.80 youth. Ⓐ place du Panthéon 75005, Ⓣ 01 44 32 18 00, Ⓦ www.monum.fr, Ⓜ Luxembourg

3. **Notre-Dame:** Get up close and personal with the gargoyles adorning the cathedral by climbing the nearly 400 steps to the top. Admission to towers: €5.50 adults, €4.50 youth; free on the first Sunday of the month, October through March. Ⓐ place du Parvis Notre-Dame 75004, Ⓣ 01 42 34 56 10, Ⓦ www.cathedraledeparis.com, Ⓜ Cité

4. **Centre Georges Pompidou:** Love or hate its gaudy exterior, the interior of this architectural marvel merits exploration—at the very least for the amazing view of the city that you get riding the escalators. Admission: €10 adults, €8 youth; free on first Sunday of every month. Ⓐ place Georges Pompidou 75004, Ⓣ 01 44 78 12 33, Ⓦ www.centrepompidou.fr, Ⓜ Rambuteau

5. **Pont des Arts:** Stand on this pedestrian bridge at sunset and take in the utterly amazing sight of the Pont Neuf, Paris's oldest bridge, spanning the tip of the Île de la Cité, one of Paris's two islands in the Seine. Ⓜ Pont Neuf

13. Sports

When you're stiff from studying or worn out from museum-hopping, you'll find that Paris offers no lack of physical activities to get your blood pumping. You can play tennis in the Jardin de Luxembourg, although courts must be reserved in advance. In the winter, a public ice-skating rink is set up in front of City Hall, while in the summer, the same space is devoted to volleyball—sand and all. In many of the city's smaller parks and gardens, you'll find Ping-Pong tables and *pétanque* courts (a Provençal game that's a lot like bocce)—just bring your own equipment.

In the realm of spectatorship, American sports junkies may go through some withdrawal—at least as far as football, hockey, basketball, and baseball are concerned. In Paris, you'll have to transfer your passions to rugby, tennis, and, of course, soccer. The French are as passionate about soccer as any other Europeans, and you'll likely find yourself following at least *Les Bleus,* the French national team, along with your new French friends.

RECREATIONAL SPORTS

Outdoor activities and adventure sports probably aren't the first things that come to mind when you think of Paris, but you might be surprised by the range of activities available—both within and outside the city. Île-de-France is relatively flat, so if you're looking for serious mountain-biking or rock-climbing, you'll have to travel to one of France's many mountainous regions.

HIKING

The *Fédération Française de la Randonnée Pédestre* (French hiking federation, www.ffrandonnee.fr) maintains thousands of kilometers of trails in the Île-de-France. Each is marked with indicators that signify the type of trail you are on: a GR (Grande Randonnée) trail traverses the country; a GRP (Sentiers de Grande Randonnée du Pays) is a regional trail; and a PR (Sentiers de Promenade) covers a smaller distance, which you can hike in a day or less. Here are a few popular spots for hiking in Paris.

Auvers-sur-Oise At Auvers-sur-Oise, PR and GR trails cut across the wheat fields and rolling hills of the landscape that inspired Vincent Van Gogh into a frenzy of production near the end of his life. Train Auvers-sur-Oise

Fontainebleau Forest Sprawling out over 62,000 acres southeast of Paris, the Fontainebleau Forest encompasses the eponymous town and spectacular Renaissance-era château and gardens. It offers dozens of day trails over a hilly landscape covered with beautiful, centuries-old trees. The types of trails in the forest are GR and PR. Train Gare de Fontainebleau-Avon

Montmorency Forest This vast forest to the northwest of Paris is popular with hikers, bikers, and horseback riders. Beware: The many PR and GR trails that cut through the chestnut trees are often muddy. Train Groslay

St-Germain-en-Laye Forest Centered around the wealthy suburb and chateau of the same name, the St-Germain-en-Laye Forest is located to the west of Paris. You can take a day hike to explore its 8,000 acres of richly varied vegetation. The types of trails in this forest are GR and PR. RER St-Germain-en-Laye

CYCLING

Paris proper offers a number of enjoyable bike routes that are insulated from the insufferable traffic that can complicate street cycling. You can ride along the city's ever-growing network of bicycle paths and around larger parks. If you're really looking to give your leg muscles a workout, you should hop on the train and head to the outlying forests of Île-de-France, which are better for serious cycling (see "Bikes" in Chapter 3 for information about renting a bike in Paris). It's a perfect day trip in the spring and summer. Here are a few cycling options.

Chevreuse Valley Get a dose of rural France in this valley just southwest of Paris. The hundreds of kilometers of trails that crisscross the land allow you to explore its many forests, rivers, lakes, and prairies. You have the possibility of renting an all-terrain bike once you get there. RER St-Rémy-les-Chevreuse

Claye-Souilly If you follow Paris's canal St-Martin, which turns into the canal de l'Ourcq, past the Parc de la Villette and out beyond the *périphérique,* or outer road, an hour or so of riding will take you to the peaceful town and forest of Claye-Souilly. Ⓜ (starting point) République, Jaurès

Promenade Plantée or Coulée Verte An elevated, lushly planted 4.5-kilometer path constructed along a former railroad line, running between the Bastille and the Bois de Vincennes. Ⓜ Bastille, Daumesnil, Porte d'Orée

ROCK CLIMBING

If you know what you're doing and already have the right equipment, you can pay a monthly or yearly fee for admission to one of the several municipal climbing walls in Paris, though you'll be required to show proof of insurance. If you're a novice, check out one of the city's *clubs d'escalade* (climbing clubs), where you can sign up to take lessons and rent equipment. The Fontainebleau Forest, sprinkled with large sandstone boulders, is probably the region's best-known spot for outdoor climbing. If you want to rent rock-climbing equipment, check out La Haute Route

(01 42 72 38 43, www.lahauteroute.com), where all-inclusive weekend equipment rental packages cost €25–€60. Here are two climbing centers in the city.

Centre Sportif Mourlon You'll pay €6 for one session; come with your own equipment. Ⓐ 19 rue Gaston de Caillavet 75015, Ⓣ 01 45 75 40 43, Ⓜ Charles Michels

Groupe Universitaire de Montagne et de Ski A seasonal membership here costs €30–€50. Ⓐ 53 rue du Moulin Vert 75014, Ⓣ 01 45 43 48 37, Ⓦ www.gumsparis.asso.fr, Ⓜ Alésia

CAMPING

When you want to sleep under the stars and your balcony just won't cut it, you can spend a weekend camping at one of the handful of sites located in Île-de-France, which are easily reachable via public transportation. Camping in the wild is forbidden in France, however, so you can't pitch your tent in any appealing field or forest, tempting as it may be. Here are some campsites and resources.

Go Sport A reasonably priced sporting goods store where you can get everything you need to prepare for your camping trip. Ⓐ Les Halles, place Carrée, Porte St-Eustache 75001, Ⓣ 01 53 00 81 70, Ⓦ www.go-sport.fr, Ⓜ Les Halles

Le Parc de la Colline This campsite offers a small grocery store and showers and rents safes, small refrigerators, and tents. Rates: €7.10 per adult. Ⓐ route de Lagny 77200 Torcy, Ⓣ 01 60 05 42 32, Ⓦ www.camping-de-la-colline.com, RER Torcy

Le Parc des Roches This campsite offers a restaurant with a terrace; a swimming pool (from June to mid-September); *pétanque*, soccer, and volleyball fields; basketball courts; and a room with Ping-Pong tables. Rates: €6.60 per adult, plus €5 per tent. Ⓐ 91530 St-Chéron, Ⓣ 01 64 56 65 50, Ⓦ www.parcdesroches.com, RER St-Chéron

ROLLERBLADING

Rollerblading is tremendously popular in Paris, with its wide sidewalks and parks and plazas. Practice your moves on Sundays by the Seine, when riverside routes are closed to automobile traffic. If you're already a seasoned skater, you can show off your tricks on the bridge by Notre-Dame, or join a hockey game at Invalides. Here are two associations to get you moving.

Paris Roller Every Friday night year-round (unless it rains), this association organizes a three-hour ride around the city with a route that changes from week to week. Rendez-vous in front of the Gare Montparnasse in the 14th *arrondissement* at 10 P.M. Ⓦ www.paris-roller.com

Rollers & Coquillages Better suited for beginners, Rollers & Coquillages organizes a three-hour Sunday afternoon outing along the same principles as Paris Roller, leaving from the boulevard Bourdon right by the Bastille in the 4th *arrondissement* at 2:30 P.M. Ⓦ www.rollers-coquillages.org

SKIING

The French Alps and the Pyrénées are among the continent's top ski destinations. Skiers will be pleasantly surprised to discover that the price of hitting the slopes in France is more affordable than it is in the United States, which helps explain the sport's extreme popularity among the French. February is traditionally the time for a ski vacation in France, and many universities offer all-inclusive packages for a weekend or a week for a great price. Here are a few ski resorts that are popular; for travel directions, visit the resorts' websites.

Alpes d'Huez Known as the "island in the sun," this is one of France's largest alpine ski resorts. As a student, you'll pay €27 for a day pass, excluding equipment rental. Ⓣ 04 76 11 44 44, Ⓦ www.alpedhuez.com

Gourette A popular Pyrénées resort, suitable for skiers of all levels. You'll pay €22 for four hours of skiing, €27 for a day, or €70 for three days, excluding equipment rental. ⓣ 05 59 05 12 17, ⓦ www.gourette.com

Tignes Another Alps resort, among the highest in Europe, and one of France's most popular with snowboarders. A one-day pass will cost you €35, excluding equipment rental. ⓣ 04 79 40 04 40, ⓦ www.tignes.net

SPECTATOR SPORTS

Paris is a world-class city when it comes to spectator sports. In addition to the Paris-based national soccer and rugby teams that inspire fanatical devotion, sporting events of international caliber are regularly played out in the city's stadiums, on its courts and tracks, and in its streets—like the Tour de France, which ends each July with the bikers speeding up and down the Champs-Élysées. For information about sports events, pick up a copy of the popular daily *L'Equipe* (www.lequipe.fr), or check out www.sports.fr.

SOCCER

European football is similar to American football only in the extreme passion it elicits from its fans. Soccer has become a particular source of national pride in France ever since the French national team— Les Bleus, as the Fédération Française de Football's team is called—won the World Cup in 1998. Paris recently held its collective breath once again as the team advanced to the final against Italy in the summer of 2006, a match that ultimately culminated in disappointment for the French.

Les Bleus play their home games at the Stade de France. Paris's own football club, the Paris St-Germain

Football Club, plays its home games at the Parc des Princes stadium. The price of tickets varies widely, but you might expect to pay around €20 for a seat.

Stade de France Ⓐ rue Francis de Pressensé 93216, St-Denis la Plaine, Ⓣ 08 92 70 09 00, Ⓦ www.stadefrance. com, Ⓜ St-Denis-Porte de Paris

Parc des Princes Ⓐ 24 rue du Commandant Guilhbaud 75016, Ⓣ 01 47 43 71 71, Ⓜ Porte de St-Cloud

RUGBY

Rugby is the sport out of which American football was born, and it is much more rough and tumble than soccer. The French National Rugby League consists of two divisions: the first-division Top 14, with fourteen teams, and the second-division Pro D2, with sixteen teams. Check out the Stade Français rugby team at the Stade Jean Bouin. You can buy tickets online at www.stade.fr, at Fnac (www.fnac.fr), or at the Virgin Megastore (www.virginmega.fr). As with soccer, tickets generally range between €10 and €50, although prices can climb much higher.

Stade Jean Bouin Ⓐ 20–40 avenue du Général Sarrail 75016, Ⓣ 01 40 71 71 00, Ⓜ Porte d'Auteuil

TENNIS

The annual French Open (officially named the *Tournoi de Roland-Garros*) provides tennis fans with two weeks of tennis bliss. Starting in late May and held at Roland-Garros, it's one of the "Grand Slam" tournaments, which also include the U.S. Open, the Australian Open, and Wimbledon. You can order tickets via third-party websites such as www.tennistickets.com, or on the official website below. Tickets can be purchased for around €100 by booking early; all unsold tickets are put up for sale at the stadium's box office about a week before the tournament begins.

Roland Garros Ⓐ 2 avenue Gordon Bennett 75016, Ⓣ 01 47 43 48 00, Ⓦ www.fft.fr/rolandgarros, Ⓜ Porte d'Auteuil

---

DISCOUNT KIOSKS

Students and anyone under twenty-nine years old can purchase reduced-price tickets to a variety of sporting and cultural events ahead of time at the following *Kiosques Paris Jeunes* (Paris youth kiosks).

Le Marais In front of the Hôtel de Ville; open 10 A.M. to 7 P.M. Monday through Friday. Ⓐ 14 rue François Miron 75004, Ⓣ 01 42 71 38 76, Ⓜ Hôtel de Ville

Champs de Mars By the Eiffel Tower; open 10 A.M. TO 6 P.M. Monday through Friday (closed Thursday mornings). Ⓐ 101 quai Branly 75015, Ⓣ 01 43 06 15 38, Ⓜ Bir Hakeim

TOUR DE FRANCE

The Tour de France takes place over three weeks in July, during which time the cyclists traverse France, and sometimes dip briefly into neighboring countries. The route varies from year to year, but it traditionally ends in Paris. It's impressive—albeit brief—to see the Tour de France racers speed by in the final moments of the event, which culminates with the pack heading up the rue de Rivoli and performing several laps up

and down the Champs-Élysées. Plant yourself behind
the barricades to catch a glimpse of the blur of bikers
as they circle around the Arc de Triomphe.

WATCHING AMERICAN SPORTS

Don't expect to find football and basketball games
on TV in your local bar. If you're aching for some
good old American sports action, you should be
able to get your fix at any number of Paris's various
anglophile and touristy bars. The chain of "Frog-
pubs" around town is a good bet:

The Frog at Bercy Village Ⓐ 25 cour St-Émilion
75012, Ⓣ 01 43 40 70 71, Ⓜ Cour St-Émilion

The Frog & British Library Ⓐ 114 avenue de
France 75013, Ⓣ 01 45 84 34 26, Ⓜ Bibliothèque

The Frog & Princess Ⓐ 9 rue Princesse 75006,
Ⓣ 01 40 51 77 38, Ⓜ St-Germain-des-Prés

The Frog & Rosbif Ⓐ 116 rue St-Denis 75002,
Ⓣ 01 42 36 34 73, Ⓜ Étienne Marcel

5 MORE REASONS TO LOVE PARIS (AS IF YOU NEEDED MORE REASONS . . .)

1. **Turkish baths:** Treat yourself to a steamy session at the Paris Mosque to revitalize in the dead of winter. Ⓐ 2 bis place du Puits de l'Ermite 75005, Ⓣ 01 45 35 97 33, Ⓜ Place Monge

2. **La Charlotte de l'Île:** Try this tea salon on Île St-Louis for storybook atmosphere and delicious chocolate and baked goods. Ⓐ 24 rue St-Louis en l'Île 75004, Ⓣ 01 43 54 25 83, Ⓜ Sully-Morland

3. **The Paris Plage:** Every summer from late July to late August, Paris closes the busy roads along the Seine and creates a "beach" in the middle of the city. Sand (more than 2,000 tons of it!), potted palm trees, and beach chairs build up the illusion.

4. **The unsung parks of Paris:** Forget Luxembourg and the Tuileries and find the parks where the ratio of tourists to Parisians drops dramatically—like la Villette and les Buttes Chaumont in the 19th *arrondissement,* André Citroën in the 15th, and Montsouris in the 14th.

5. **Subsidized apartments:** The French state will help subsidize your apartment, even though you're foreign. For further information and application forms, go to the website of the Caisse d'Allocations Familiales. Ⓦ www.caf.fr.

14. Cultural Activities

The number of artistic, musical, cinematic, literary, and theatrical events going on at any moment in Paris is astonishing. Just flip through a copy of *L'Officiel des Spectacles* or *Pariscope,* weekly cultural guides that are available at any news kiosk, and you'll see that you could easily spend the better part of your time in Paris attending countless exhibitions, concerts, and festivals.

France is extremely proud of its artistic heritage and is determined to maintain its relevance. Substantial French public funds are devoted to the arts, which allows for free cultural events throughout the city and country and keeps museum and show prices reasonable—especially for young people and students, who are eligible for a variety of discounts. You have to work hard to be bored in Paris!

ART MUSEUMS AND GALLERIES

Paris is saturated with world-renowned galleries and museums. Many of these museum structures are works of art themselves, exquisite and innovative landmarks in a city that otherwise tends toward architectural homogeneity. Discounted tickets are generally available for students and young people, and free entry to all national museums is also extended to the public on the first Sunday of every month. Just remember that most museums are closed on Mondays or Tuesdays. Here are some of the must-see options; you can find a comprehensive list of museums and galleries at www.parisinfo.com/en.

Centre Georges Pompidou One of the best hang-out spots in Paris, this massive, playful structure houses the national collection of modern art, numerous temporary exhibitions, a library, a bookstore, a design store, a café, and a chic restaurant. The adjacent plaza, filled with students and young Parisians of every stripe, is among the most colorful in the city. **Admission:** €10 for adults, €8 for anyone age twenty-five and under; free on the first Sunday of every month. **Hours:** Open 11:00 A.M. to 10 P.M. Wednesday through Monday; closed Tuesdays and May 1. Ⓐ place Georges Pompidou 75004, Ⓣ 01 44 78 12 33, Ⓦ www.centrepompidou.fr, Ⓜ Rambuteau

Cité de la Musique Set in the exceptional Parc de la Villette, this is an interactive space where you can attend exhibitions, concerts, conferences, and courses related to music from all over the globe. **Admission:** €6.10 adults; €4.80 students. **Hours:** Open 12:00 A.M. to 6:00 P.M Tuesday through Saturday, and 10:00 A.M. to 6:00 P.M. Sunday; closed Mondays. Ⓐ 221 avenue Jean Jaurès 75019, Ⓣ 01 44 84 44 84, Ⓦ www.cite-musique.fr, Ⓜ Porte de Pantin

Grand Palais Constructed for the 1900 World's Fair and known for its intricately beautiful art nouveau ironwork, this edifice hosts several international exhibitions of outstanding caliber each year, ranging from ancient Indian civilization to the art of Walt Disney. **Admission:** €10 adults; €8 students. **Hours:** 10:00 A.M. to 8:00 P.M. Sunday through Monday, 10:00 A.M. to 10:00 P.M. Wednesdays, 10:00 A.M. to 8:00 P.M. Thursday through Saturday; closed Tuesdays, May 1, and December 25. Ⓐ 3 avenue du Général-Eisenhower 75008, Ⓣ 01 44 13 17 30, Ⓦ www.rmn.fr/galeriesnationalesdugrandpalais, Ⓜ Champs-Élysées-Clemenceau

Louvre Any number of superlatives cannot begin to sum up the splendors of the Louvre, whose collections, contained within a sprawling one-time fortress and castle, span civilizations and centuries. Its vast collections house some of the most famous artwork from across the globe, including the *Mona Lisa, Venus de Milo,* and *The Virgin and Child with St. Anne.* **Admission:** €8.50 for adults; reduced price of €6 from 6:00 P.M. to 9:45 P.M. on Wednesdays and Fridays; free admission for anyone under age twenty-six from 6:00 P.M. to 9:45 P.M. every Friday; free on the first Sunday of every month. **Hours:** 9:00 A.M. to 6:00 P.M. Sunday through Monday, Thursday, and Saturday; 9:00 A.M. to 10:00 P.M. Wednesday and Friday; closed Tuesdays, January 1, May 1 and 8, and December 25. Ⓐ Located between the Seine and rue de Rivoli, and from rue du Louvre to place de la Concorde 75001, Ⓣ 01 40 20 50 50, Ⓦ www.louvre.fr, Ⓜ Palais Royal-Musée du Louvre

Musée d'Orsay This converted train station principally exhibits European art of the nineteenth and twentieth centuries and contains one of the most extensive collections of Impressionist works in the world. Join the crowds to see Monet, Renoir, and other favorites, as well as works by Toulouse-Lautrec, Rodin, and Camille Corot. **Admission:** €9 for adults; €7 for anyone age twenty-five and under, as well as on Sundays and after 4:15 P.M. on every day except Thursday, when it's €7 after 8 P.M.; free admission on the first Sunday of every month. **Hours:** 9:30 A.M. to 6:00 P.M. Sunday, Tuesday, and Wednesday, and Friday through Saturday; 9:30 A.M. to 9:45 P.M. Thursday; closed Mondays, January 1, May 1, and December 25. Ⓐ 1 rue de la Légion d'honneur 75007, Ⓣ 01 40 49 48 14, Ⓦ www.musee-orsay.fr, Ⓜ Solférino, RER Musée d'Orsay

Musée du Quai Branly The most recent feat of renowned French architect Jean Nouvel, this astonishing museum is devoted to non-Western cultures, displaying art and artifacts of Africa, the Americas, Asia, and Oceania. **Admission:** €8.50 adults; €6 students. **Hours:** 10:00 A.M. to 6:30 P.M. Tuesday and Wednesday, and Friday through Sunday; 10:00 A.M. to 9:30 P.M. Thursday; closed Mondays, January 1, May 1, and December 25. Ⓐ 37 quai Branly 75007, Ⓣ 01 56 61 70 00, Ⓦ www.quaibranly.fr, Ⓜ Iéna/Bir-Hakeim

GUIDED SIGHTSEEING TOURS

There's no substitute for exploring the city on your own, and Paris is a city that begs to be wandered through—whether you're on your way somewhere or just want to take in the sights. But if you're looking for a different way to spend an afternoon or have out-of-town guests to entertain, you'll find plenty of companies that organize guided tours around town on foot, by bus, or by boat. Here are a few of the most popular options.

Boats One of the most picturesque ways to see Paris is to take a relaxing float down the Seine in a Bâteau Mouche (Ⓦ www.bateauxmouches.com) or a Bâteau Parisien (Ⓦ www.bateauxparisiens.com). These and other sightseeing boats will take you up and down the river for around €10, pointing out the sights as you go.

Cityrama Cityrama's tours come in the form of giant yellow double-decker buses, with recorded commentary available in thirteen languages (headphones included). This is a comprehensive, though expensive, way to see the sights. The cost is about €25 for a ninety-minute tour. Ⓦ www.ecityrama.com

Paris Walks This walking tour company offers strolls along various routes at fixed times each week. Its English-language tours, such as "Hemingway" and "Writers of the Left Bank," attract both tourists and locals. There's generally no need to sign up in advance. Walks last about two hours and cost around €10. Ⓦ http://ourworld.compuserve.com/homepages/pariswalking

PERFORMING ARTS

Parisians are generally enthusiastic patrons of the performing arts. While there's no central, Broadway-like theater district in the city, you'll find plenty of performance spaces great and small in every neighborhood. In Paris, unsold tickets may be purchased at half price or for a reduced price fifteen minutes to an hour before the performance, although you'll generally have to stand in line quite a bit in advance. Be sure to ask whether there are any student discounts when you buy tickets.

OPERA/BALLET

Paris has two opera houses: the ornate, nineteenth-century Palais Garnier (also called the Opéra Garnier), with its impressive, Chagall-painted ceiling; and the vast, modern Opéra Bastille, completed in 1989 as part of the urban renewal of east Paris. Both venues host operas as well as concerts and a wide range of dance performances by both French and international troupes (the world-renowned Paris Opera Ballet is based at the Palais Garnier). The Théâtre du Châtelet is another highly respected site for opera, as well as other theatrical performances.

Opéra National de Paris (encompasses both the Palais Garnier and the Opéra Bastille) Ⓐ 120 rue de Lyon 75014, Ⓣ 08 92 89 90 90, Ⓦ www.operadeparis.fr, Ⓜ Bastille

Théâtre du Châtelet Ⓐ 1 place du Châtelet 75001, Ⓣ 01 40 28 28 40, Ⓦ www.chatelet-theatre.com, Ⓜ Châtelet

THEATER

While going to the theater in Paris may prove challenging if your French isn't yet up to par, a night out on the town in a beautiful venue such as the Comédie Française is an experience that transcends linguistic hurdles. The theater is grand, with an imposing, column-laden exterior crowned with golden statues. Additionally, you can generally find a handful of contemporary and experimental plays being performed around town, such as in the Théâtre de la Bastille and Théâtre des Bouffes du Nord.

Comédie Française, Salle Richelieu Ⓐ place Colette 75001, Ⓣ 08 25 10 16 80, Ⓦ www.comedie-francaise.fr, Ⓜ Palais Royal-Musée du Louvre

Théâtre de la Bastille Ⓐ 76 rue de la Roquette 75011, Ⓣ 01 43 57 42 14, Ⓦ www.theatre-bastille.com, Ⓜ Voltaire

Théâtre des Bouffes du Nord Ⓐ 37 bis boulevard de la Chapelle 75010, Ⓣ 01 46 07 34 50, Ⓦ www.bouffesdunord.com, Ⓜ La Chapelle

THEATER IN ENGLISH

Got a thirst for theater but want to leave your French dictionary at home for a change? Paris has a bilingual theater troupe called the Dear Conjunction Theatre Company that performs in both English and French, so your craving for drama can be satisfied even if your French needs a little (or more than a little) work. The company performs at the Sudden Theatre.

Dear Conjunction Theatre Company Ⓐ 6 rue Arthur-Rozier 75019, Ⓣ 01 42 41 69 65, Ⓜ Jourdain, Place des Fêtes

Sudden Theatre Ⓐ 14 bis rue St-Isaure 75018, Ⓣ 01 42 62 35 00, Ⓜ Jules-Joffrin, Simplon

CLASSICAL MUSIC

Both of the city's opera houses host classical music performances in addition to dance and opera (see "Opera/Ballet"), and there are numerous other venues that welcome orchestras and musicians from near and far. A notable auditorium is at the Cité de la Musique in the Parc de la Villette, which hosts music from around the world. And the Théâtre des Champs-Élysées is a renowned and prestigious traditional recital hall.

Cité de la Musique Ⓐ 221 avenue Jean-Jaurès 75019, Ⓣ 01 44 84 45 45, Ⓦ www.cite-musique.fr, Ⓜ Porte de Pantin

Théâtre des Champs-Élysées Ⓐ 15 avenue Montaigne 75008, Ⓣ 01 49 52 50 50, Ⓦ www.theatrechampselysees.fr, Ⓜ Alma-Marceau

DISCOUNT KIOSKS

Discounted tickets to performing arts and sports events are available at *Kiosques Paris Jeunes* (Paris youth kiosks) throughout Paris (see Chapter 13, "Sports," for locations). Additionally, there are two *Kiosques Moitié Prix* (half-price kiosks) where reduced-price tickets are available on the day of the performance. Both are open 12:30 P.M. to 7:45 P.M. Tuesday through Friday and 12:30 P.M. to 3:45 P.M. Sunday.

Kiosque de la Madeleine Ⓐ 15 place de la Madeleine 75008, Ⓜ Madeleine

Kiosque Montparnasse Ⓐ parvis de la Gare Montparnasse 75015, Ⓜ Montparnasse-Bienvenüe

FILMS

Paris has been a mecca for cinephiles since the Lumière brothers, the city's homegrown filmmaking pioneers, first wowed Parisian audiences in the late nineteenth century. The Latin Quarter's legendary, minimalist art houses coexist with the ever-encroaching giant multiplex chains. Verify whether your movie of choice is being shown in *version originale* (V.O., or subtitled in French) or *version française* (V.F., the dubbed French version). The city's filmgoers tend to snub dubbed screenings in favor of subtitles, so in most cases you won't have to compromise your moviegoing experience by listening to Jack Nicholson with a French accent. New releases generally open on Wednesdays.

MOVIE THEATERS

You'll generally pay between €6 and €9 for a movie ticket, or between €5 and €6.50 with a student discount. Many theaters charge a set price of €5 for showings before noon and offer discounted ticket prices on Wednesdays. You'll also find slightly cheaper prices at independent theaters (as opposed to the bigger chains like UGC, Gaumont, and MK2), which receive subsidies from the government. Following is a mix of indie and mainstream theaters.

La Cinémathèque Française Specializes in foreign films. Ⓐ 51 rue de Bercy 75012, Ⓣ 01 71 19 33 33, Ⓦ www.cinematheque.fr, Ⓜ Bercy

Le Champo Plays classic films and film series, such as retrospectives of certain directors. Ⓐ 51 rue des Écoles 75005, Ⓣ 08 92 68 69 21, Ⓦ www.lechampo.com, Ⓜ St-Michel

MK2 Quai de Seine/Quai de Loire Shows Hollywood blockbusters. Ⓐ 14 quai de Seine/7 quai de Loire 75019, Ⓣ 08 92 68 47 07 or 08 92 69 84 84, Ⓦ http://mk2.fr, Ⓜ Jaurès, Stalingrad

FILM FESTIVALS

Many Parisian movie houses regularly run spontaneous, low-key festivals ranging from specific directors to genres like Italian neorealism or Bollywood. These screenings are scheduled alongside normally programmed new releases and second runs. In addition, prominent annual festivals occur at different venues (including many museums). Numerous free and cheap open-air and indoor festivals are also organized in the summer. The following is a smattering of festivals.

Cinéma du Réel An international documentary film festival organized by the Bibliothèque Publique d'Information that is held in the Centre Georges Pompidou every March. Ⓦ www.cinereel.org

L'Étrange Festival A festival organized by the Forum des Images in the late summer, devoted to experimental, alternative cinema and marginalized or obscure directors and performers. Ⓦ www.etrangefestival.com

Les Rencontres Internationales de Cinéma à Paris A festival that takes place over two weeks in June and July, during which hundreds of independent, international films are screened in a dozen theaters throughout the city. Ⓦ www.pariscinema.org

---

CHEAP CLASSES

The *Mairie de Paris* (the city council) sponsors a wide range of language, creative, and other types of classes that are among the most popular and cheapest (ranging from about €25 to €450 for a semester- or yearlong course) in the city. Spots go quickly, and sign-up begins September 1. Pick up an application at your local Mairie or at l'Hôtel de Ville (see the Appendix for Mairie contact information for each *arrondissement*). Go to www.paris.fr for further details.

HOLIDAYS

A traditionally Catholic country, France staunchly, if secularly, celebrates a host of Catholic holidays. Mostly, these holidays are an excuse to slip away to the countryside or the seashore. Nonreligious, national celebrations are generally observed in the traditional French manner, with fanfare, fireworks, military, and processions. There are eleven official holidays, religious and secular, per year in France. Here is just a sampling of the many holidays that dot the Parisian calendar.

Fête de la Chandeleur (Candlemas): February 2 This traditionally Christian celebration is observed by making crêpes and is a great excuse to have a crêpe party.

Pâques (Easter): March or April According to the French tradition, bells, rather than bunnies, are charged with delivering Easter eggs and other treats. Easter is lengthened into a three-day weekend, as the following Monday is treated as a public holiday.

Fête du Travail (Labor Day): May 1 France's Labor Day is observed with a syndicate-led march leaving from the place de la République in the afternoon.

Fête de la Victoire 1945 (World War II Victory Day): May 8 The Allied victory of 1945 is commemorated each year with official military ceremonies paying homage to veterans and members of the Résistance.

Ascension (Ascension): May This Catholic holiday celebrates the ascension of Jesus into heaven forty days after Easter.

Pentecôte (Pentecost): May Pentecost is observed on the Sunday seven weeks after Easter, and the following Monday has traditionally been given off as a public holiday.

Fête Nationale (Bastille Day): July 14 French Independence Day is celebrated on the anniversary of the taking of the Bastille July 14, 1789, an act of popular resistance to the absolutism of the French monarchy.

Assomption (Assumption): August 15 This holiday recognizes Mary's ascension into heaven, which is celebrated by all Catholics.

Toussaint (All Saints): November 1 All Saints is celebrated in honor of all of the saints of the Roman Catholic Church. It's a tradition to go to cemeteries to pay visits to loved ones who have passed away.

Armistice 1918 (Veterans Day): November 11 This is the anniversary of the signing of the accords between Germany and the Allied powers, which put an end to World War I at 11:00 A.M. on the eleventh day of the eleventh month of 1918.

End-of-the-Year Festivities: December 25 and January 31
Noël (Christmas) and la St-Sylvestre (New Year's Eve) are increasingly celebrated in a commercially crazed fashion. Gastronomically speaking, the French typically consume shellfish and seafood (notably, bucket loads of oysters).

5 AFFORDABLE DAY TRIPS

1. **Chartres:** The town of Chartres, an hour southwest of Paris, is home to the Chartres cathedral, France's largest Gothic cathedral. Do as the religious pilgrims did and walk the labyrinth carved into the floor on your knees. Take a train from Gare de Montparnasse; the price of a round-trip ticket ranges from €12 to €25.

2. **Giverny:** Visit Monet's home and gardens in this village 50 miles west of Paris, where the Impressionist master painted his beloved water lilies. Take a train from Gare St-Lazare; a round-trip ticket costs €12 to €23.

3. **Reims:** Ninety miles or so northeast of Paris lies the Champagne region's largest city. There you can tour the headquarters of the finest French producers of bubbly and visit the cathedral of Reims, where France's kings were crowned. Take a train from Gare de l'Est; a round-trip ticket costs €22 to €44.

4. **Senlis:** This town in the Oise area to the north of Paris contains Roman ruins, one of France's best-preserved medieval walled cities, and the cathedral Notre-Dame de Senlis. Take a train from Gare du Nord; a round-trip ticket costs €4 to €8.

5. **Versailles:** Soak in the splendor of the seventeenth-century palace of the Sun King, to the southwest of Paris, about a half-hour train ride away. The palace is stunning, as are the extensive gardens. You can get there on the RER C; a round-trip ticket costs €5.60.

15. Eating Out

While Lyon, France's second-biggest city, is considered to be the capital of traditional French dining, Paris escapes category when it comes to cuisine. Today, you'll find traditional French bistros and brasseries firmly entrenched next to restaurants serving up West Indian acras, Colombian ajiaco, Spanish tapas, Moroccan tagines, Vietnamese nems, Japanese soba, and Sri Lankan seeni sambol.

One element of French dining that takes some getting used to is the precise order of the courses: appetizer/soup, entrée, salad, cheese, dessert, coffee. (Try ordering a *café* with your quiche, just to witness your waiter's perplexed reaction.) The key to surviving the marathon is the small quantities. Mealtimes, too, are rigid: Lunch is generally served between noon and 2 P.M., while dinner generally starts around 8 P.M. Most restaurants close between the two meals, but many cafés and brasseries offer standard dishes such as omelettes, onion soup, and *croques* (hot sandwiches) all day.

In this chapter, we use ✅ to indicate spots where you can expect to spend €10 or less for lunch and around €15 for dinner (main course plus a beer or a glass of house wine).

DINNER WITH FRIENDS

Paris is full of cool spots to share a night out with friends, where you can eat and drink in high style without breaking the bank. Many restaurants accept reservations—essential if you have a large party or if you're headed to a popular spot on a Friday or Saturday night. At some restaurants, because of layout or lack of space, you may be asked to share a table with other people.

Ave Maria Offers deliciously creative, reasonably priced, and varied cuisines from all over the world, from India to Brazil, as well as a beautiful waitstaff and eclectic decor. Ⓐ 1 rue Jacquard 75011, Ⓣ 01 47 00 61 73, Ⓜ Oberkampf

Ⓥ **Café de l'Industrie** A Bastille institution that offers simple, classic French fare in a unique setting filled with artwork. Ⓐ 16 rue St-Sabin 75011, Ⓣ 01 47 00 13 53, Ⓜ Bastille, Breguet-Sabin

La Cave de L'Os à Moelle Serves traditional French food family-style. Ⓐ 181 rue de Lourmel 75015, Ⓣ 08 26 10 06 01, Ⓜ Duplex

Le Chaland Serves excellent-quality, simple French cuisine, such as sandwiches made with duck terrine (like *pâté*), in an intimate atmosphere on the canal St-Martin. Ⓐ 2 passage Delessert 75010, Ⓣ 01 40 05 18 68, Ⓜ Château Landon

Les Crocs Offers traditional French food prepared from scratch with fresh ingredients. Ⓐ 14 rue de Cotte 75012, Ⓣ 01 43 46 63 63, Ⓜ Ledru-Rollin

Ⓥ **Le Fleuve Rouge** Features a globally inspired menu and a homey, eclectically decorated restaurant. It's in a village-like neighborhood in the 19th *arrondissement*. Ⓐ 1 rue Pradier 75019, Ⓣ 01 42 06 25 04, Ⓜ Buttes-Chaumont

Ⓥ **Menelik** Offers excellent Ethiopian food, served in the traditional style: on a large communal platter with pieces of flat bread to eat it with. Ⓐ 4 rue Sauffroy 75017, Ⓣ 01 46 27 00 82, Ⓜ Brochant

Ⓥ **Pho Banh Cuon 14** A crowded Chinatown restaurant where you can enjoy a steaming bowl of pho. Ⓐ 129 avenue de Choisy 75013, Ⓣ 01 45 83 61 15, Ⓜ Tolbiac

Ⓥ **Le Verre Luisant** Offers traditional, hearty French dishes such as *poulet fermier* (a European-style chicken) with potatoes and nice salads at reasonable prices. Ⓐ 64 rue de la Verrerie 75004, Ⓣ 01 42 72 67 63, Ⓜ Rambuteau, Hôtel de Ville

✓ Les Voisins Serves Spanish sangria, tapas, and a delicious *crema catalana* in a spirited environment. Ⓐ 27 rue Yves Toudic 75010, ① 01 42 49 36 58, Ⓜ République, Jacques Bonsergent

---

DÉFENSE DE FUMER (NO SMOKING)

It used to be that sitting down at a café in Paris was synonymous with lighting up, and nonsmoking rules in restaurants and cafés were only half-heartedly enforced. In 2007, a new law took effect that bans smoking in workplaces, hospitals, and other public places, with a hefty fine for disobeying. Smoking will be banned from bars and restaurants beginning in 2008.

DINNER WITH FAMILY

Dinner with visiting family is the perfect excuse for testing out some of the city's finer restaurants, which can be pricey but are generally worth the splurge (especially when parents are taking care of the tab). Out-of-towners may be eager to try out some traditional French fare, which you'll find everywhere—in restaurants of variable quality. Here are a few reliable options.

Le Café Marly Features sometimes-experimental renditions of traditional French dishes in a sumptuous environment under the arches of the Louvre. Ⓐ Palais du Louvre 75001, ① 01 49 26 06 60, Ⓜ Palais Royal-Musée du Louvre

---

Chez Janou Serves Provençale cuisine, including a wide selection of *pastis* (an aniseed-flavored aperitif), just behind the places des Vosges. Ⓐ 2 rue Roger Verlomme 75003, ① 01 42 72 28 41, Ⓜ Chemin Vert

---

L'Ébauchoir Prepares traditional French cuisine in a relaxed setting. Ⓐ 43–45 rue de Cîteaux 75012, ① 01 43 42 49 31, Ⓜ Faidherbe-Chaligny

---

Fish La Boissonnerie Specializes in perfectly prepared fish.
Ⓐ 69 rue de Seine 75006, Ⓣ 01 43 54 34 69, Ⓜ Mabillon

La Grille Offers a cozy, old-world atmosphere, with an incredible turbot and *beurre blanc* (a butter sauce) as its masterpiece. Ⓐ 80 rue du Faubourg Poissonnière 75010, Ⓣ 01 47 70 89 73, Ⓜ Poissonnière

Marmite Bazar Traditional cuisine is reinvented with an exotic flair in this warm, colorful restaurant. Ⓐ 14 rue Bochart de Saron 75009, Ⓣ 01 48 78 51 47, Ⓜ Anvers

Ⓥ **Parnasse 138** Features a fresh, reasonably priced, and varied menu inspired by the southwest of France, where the cuisine is notable for its rich delicacies (think *foie gras* and *confit de canard*). Ⓐ 138 boulevard Montparnasse 75014, Ⓣ 01 43 20 47 87, Ⓜ Port Royal

La Plage Parisienne Appropriately enough, fish is the high point on the menu at this restaurant located on a barge docked on the banks of the Seine. Ⓐ Port de Javel Haut 75015, Ⓣ 01 40 59 41 00, Ⓜ Charles Michel

Le Tambour Enjoy classic fare in an eclectic, lively, friendly setting that's reminiscent of another era. Ⓐ 41 rue Montmartre 75002, Ⓣ 01 42 33 06 90, Ⓜ Les Halles, Sentier

Voyage au Siam The welcome is warm in this restaurant specializing in beautifully presented traditional Thai food. Diners even have access to a small library. Ⓐ 60–62 rue St-Maur 75011, Ⓣ 01 47 00 46 87, Ⓜ Rue Saint-Maur

REGIONAL CUISINES

Each region in France has its own culinary specialties, characterized by the use of local ingredients. Provence features Mediterranean-style cuisine, and the southeast is Italianesque in its use of sun-loving vegetables, herbs, garlic, and olive oil. Sauerkraut and sausage reign supreme in Alsace-Lorraine, near Germany. The northwest, particularly Normandy, is dairy territory, while Brittany is known for savory *galettes* (crêpes). The southwest is renowned for duck and foie gras production.

DATE SPOTS

There is no shortage of great date spots in Paris, whether you're looking for traditional, romantic, lounge-by-candlelight-type place; a low-key spot that's conducive to conversation; or a place that, in and of itself, is a conversation-starter, in case you're nervous about finding something to talk about. Do as the French do and sit side-by-side, rather than facing each other, for instant intimacy. Here are a few places to get your romance on.

Au Village Offers authentic Senegalese fare in a cozy setting. Reservations on weekends are essential. Ⓐ 86 avenue Parmentier 75011, Ⓣ 01 43 57 18 95, Ⓜ Parmentier

China Club Features elegant, colonial-style décor, inviting leather sofas, dim lighting, and refined Chinese cuisine. Ⓐ 50 rue de Charenton 75012, Ⓣ 08 26 10 11 59, Ⓦ http://china club.cc, Ⓜ Ledru-Rollin

Le Georges Features an incredible panoramic view of Paris from the terrace—as well as inflated prices thanks to its chic reputation. Ⓐ Centre Georges Pompidou 6ème étage 75004, Ⓣ 01 44 78 47 99, Ⓦ www.centrepompidou.fr, Ⓜ Rambuteau

Hôtel du Nord A trendy yet classy establishment on the banks of the canal St-Martin that offers candlelit ambiance and a cool terrace. Ⓐ 102 quai de Jemmapes 75010, Ⓣ 01 40 40 78 78, Ⓦ www.hoteldunord.org, Ⓜ Goncourt

Au Jardin Stands out as a quiet and intimate refuge for fine dining in a busy neighborhood of mediocre restaurants. Ⓐ 15 rue Gît-le-Cœur 75006, Ⓣ 01 43 26 29 44, Ⓜ St-Michel

Le Lamarck Specializes in Corsican cuisine. It's owned by a very nice couple—the husband often offers his considerable musical talents along with the meal. Ⓐ 8 rue Lamarck 75018, Ⓣ 01 53 41 01 60, Ⓜ Lamarck-Caulaincourt

Mai Thai Offers excellent Thai cuisine in an elegant Marais setting. Ⓐ 24 bis rue St-Gilles 75003, Ⓣ 01 42 72 18 77, Ⓜ Chemin Vert

El Palenque An Argentinian steakhouse that offers a selection of fine South American wines. Ⓐ 5 rue de la Montagne-Sainte-Geneviève 75005, Ⓣ 01 43 54 08 99, Ⓜ Maubert-Mutualité

Restaurant de la Mosquée de Paris Features an extravagant interior and traditional North African *couscous, tagines,* mint tea, and honey-drenched pastries. Ⓐ 39 rue Geoffroy St-Hilaire 75005, Ⓣ 01 43 31 38 20, Ⓦ www.mosquee-de-paris. net, Ⓜ Censier-Daubenton, Jussieu

Le Winch Features expertly prepared seafood in a marine-inspired atmosphere. Ⓐ 44 rue Damrémont 75018, Ⓣ 01 42 23 04 63, Ⓜ Lamarck-Caulaincourt

LATE-NIGHT FOOD

Paris bars tend to close at 2 A.M., but in lively neighborhoods, you can always find a crêpe or sandwich stand to combat those post-drinking hunger pangs. If you're on the prowl for a sit-down joint to grab a last drink or meal, however, you may have to do a bit of walking. A handful of all-night places are concentrated around Les Halles, while the area around the Bastille is also a good bet for places open into the wee hours.

Bar Brasserie La Bastille A large establishment ideally situated for a late-night/early-morning drink or bite to eat. Ⓐ 8 place de la Bastille 75011, Ⓣ 01 43 07 79 95, Ⓜ Bastille

Café Rey A welcoming place that serves up classic French fare 24/7. Ⓐ 130 rue de la Roquette 75011, Ⓣ 01 43 79 77 26, Ⓜ Voltaire

Au Pied de Cochon A Parisian institution that offers good French food and drinks twenty-four hours a day. It dates back to the days when Les Halles was the city's central food market. Ⓐ 6 rue Coquillière 75001, Ⓣ 01 40 13 77 00, Ⓦ www. pieddecochon.com, Ⓜ Les Halles

Le Starcooker A Marais bar/restaurant that offers comfy sofas and snacks as the sun rises in the city. Ⓐ 32 rue des Archives 75004, Ⓣ 01 42 77 12 17, Ⓜ Hôtel de Ville

La Tour Montlhéry A cozy, typically Parisian bistro that offers good meals at all hours of the day and night. Ⓐ 5 rue Prouvaires 75001, Ⓣ 01 42 36 21 82, Ⓜ Les Halles

VEGETARIAN

The Paris restaurant scene is diverse enough that you should have no trouble avoiding traditional carnivore-oriented French fare. Restaurants that are strictly vegetarian, however, are not that common. Here are three good bets.

Au Grain de Folie A postage stamp-size vegetarian restaurant serving up tasty organic specialties that are made to order. Ⓐ 24 rue de la Vieuville 75018, Ⓣ 01 42 58 15 57, Ⓜ Abbesses

La Pharmacie: A strictly organic, vegetarian café-restaurant whose lovely interior is complete with cozy armchairs and an inviting back salon. Ⓐ 22 rue Jean-Pierre Timbaud 75011, Ⓣ 01 43 38 04 99, Ⓜ Oberkampf

Le Potager du Marais Original, organic vegetarian cuisine attracts those looking for something out of the ordinary to this charming Marais establishment. Ⓐ 22 rue Rambuteau 75003, Ⓣ 01 42 74 24 66, Ⓜ Rambuteau

LUNCH/FOOD TO GO

If you're in a rush and on a budget, turn to one of the bakeries or sandwich and crêpe stands that appear on nearly every block of the city, as well as *traiteurs asiatiques* (fast-food Asian restaurants). Falafel or *pho* (Vietnamese soup) are other good bets for a quick lunch. If you want a sit-down lunch, many restaurants offer fixed-price menus that allow you to order an appetizer and entrée or entrée and dessert for a very reasonable price. Here are a few reliable places for lunch in Paris.

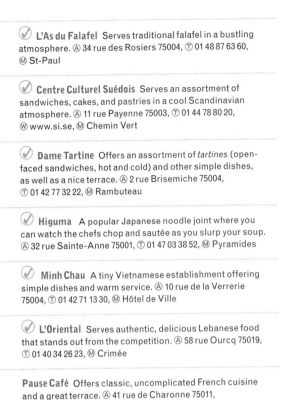

✅ **L'As du Falafel** Serves traditional falafel in a bustling atmosphere. Ⓐ 34 rue des Rosiers 75004, Ⓣ 01 48 87 63 60, Ⓜ St-Paul

✅ **Centre Culturel Suédois** Serves an assortment of sandwiches, cakes, and pastries in a cool Scandinavian atmosphere. Ⓐ 11 rue Payenne 75003, Ⓣ 01 44 78 80 20, Ⓦ www.si.se, Ⓜ Chemin Vert

✅ **Dame Tartine** Offers an assortment of *tartines* (open-faced sandwiches, hot and cold) and other simple dishes, as well as a nice terrace. Ⓐ 2 rue Brisemiche 75004, Ⓣ 01 42 77 32 22, Ⓜ Rambuteau

✅ **Higuma** A popular Japanese noodle joint where you can watch the chefs chop and sautée as you slurp your soup. Ⓐ 32 rue Sainte-Anne 75001, Ⓣ 01 47 03 38 52, Ⓜ Pyramides

✅ **Minh Chau** A tiny Vietnamese establishment offering simple dishes and warm service. Ⓐ 10 rue de la Verrerie 75004, Ⓣ 01 42 71 13 30, Ⓜ Hôtel de Ville

✅ **L'Oriental** Serves authentic, delicious Lebanese food that stands out from the competition. Ⓐ 58 rue Ourcq 75019, Ⓣ 01 40 34 26 23, Ⓜ Crimée

Pause Café Offers classic, uncomplicated French cuisine and a great terrace. Ⓐ 41 rue de Charonne 75011, Ⓣ 01 48 06 80 33, Ⓜ Bastille, Ledru-Rollin

Le Petit Marcel Specializes in simple, authentic, high-quality cuisine for a low price. Ⓐ 65 rue Rambuteau 75004, Ⓣ 01 48 87 10 20, Ⓜ Rambuteau

✅ **Pizza César** Offers what some say is the best pizza in Paris (it's Italian-style, which means it has a thin, crispy crust). Ⓐ 81 boulevard St-Marcel 75013, Ⓣ 01 43 31 68 60, Ⓜ Gobelins

✅ **Tienda Nueva** A Colombian grocer/eating joint that offers tamales, fajitas, empanadas, and other traditional specialties that you can eat at the bar or take out. Ⓐ 57 rue Rodier 75009, Ⓣ 01 45 26 11 80, Ⓜ Anvers

TIPPING IN RESTAURANTS

Service in French restaurants is not overly attentive, and you are guaranteed only two visits by your waiter: the first to take your order, and the second to deliver your food. A service charge of about 15 percent is included in your bill—it's factored into the price of your food. If you're happy with your meal and the service, you can leave an additional tip of a euro or two on the table.

5 *FREE* WAYS TO SPEND AN EVENING WITH FRIENDS

1. **Maison de Radio France:** Check out one of many radio show recordings open to the public at this building housing France's seven public stations. Check whether telephone reservations are accepted. Ⓐ 116 avenue du Président Kennedy 75016, Ⓣ 01 56 40 22 22, Ⓦ www.radiofrance.fr, Ⓜ Passy

2. **Centre Georges Pompidou's bookshop:** Many an hour can be whiled away at this cool bookshop, which specializes in artsy books. Ⓐ 19 rue Beaubourg 75004, Ⓣ 01 44 78 12 33, Ⓦ www.centrepompidou.fr, Ⓜ Rambuteau

3. **Ping-Pong and *pétanque*:** Ping-Pong tables and *pétanque* courts are in the center of the boulevard Richard Lenoir around the Richard Lenoir Métro station; *pétanque* courts are along the banks of canal de l'Ourcq and by the Buttes-Chaumont on rue Botzaris.

4. **Picnics:** Pack a *baguette,* a wheel of *camembert, and* a bottle of wine and head to the banks of canal St-Martin, one of Paris's most popular picnic destinations. Ⓜ République, Gare de l'Est, or Jacques Bonsergent

5. **Free concerts:** On any given night in Paris there are free classical concerts in many of the city's centuries-old cathedrals. Check out the weekly magazines *L'Officiel des Spectacles* and *Pariscope,* which you can buy at any newsstand, for listings.

16. Night Life

There's something happening in Paris seven nights a week, but the city's night life is not as raucous as that of other European capitals and big cities. This is not to say that Parisians don't know how to party: There are dozens of renowned (and ritzy) clubs, but the French proclivity for spending evenings of prolonged conversation among friends means that bars tend to dominate the going-out scene—that is, in the absence of get-togethers at someone's apartment or, weather permitting, outdoor gatherings in parks or on the banks of the Seine.

While the French are among the world's highest consumers of alcohol, the country's relaxed, permissive attitude toward drinking means that young people don't tend to overdo it. Parisians are definitely not prone to public drunkenness. Be aware that vast stretches of the city are entirely dead after dark, and few bars stay open after 2 A.M. However, clubs often keep their doors open all night long on the weekends.

In this chapter, we use ⊘ to indicate places that don't charge a cover. How much you spend really depends on how much you drink.

BARS

Paris has a huge population of international students and young people, and thus a huge population of bar-hopping night owls. There are loads of anglophone bars (English, Irish, Australian, American), many of which are touristy or full of Parisians looking to pick up fresh-faced young English-speakers, and many of which actually attract a diverse local clientele.

Likewise, there are many French bars that are patronized by an international crowd, be they American students or otherwise.

Bar Ourcq One of the best spots in the city for an outdoor drink, where you can sip your beer right on the bank of the canal. Ⓐ 68 quai de la Loire 75019, Ⓣ 01 42 40 12 26, Ⓜ Laumière

Le Baron Rouge Cool neighborhood wine bar where you can fill your liter straight from the barrel and nibble on a farm-fresh selection of cheeses and charcuterie. Ⓐ 1 rue Théophile Roussel 75012, Ⓣ 01 43 43 14 32, Ⓜ Ledru-Rollin

Le Bombardier A bar in the heart of the Latin Quarter where students gather to drink imported beers, play darts, and participate in trivia contests. Ⓐ 2 place du Panthéon 75005, Ⓣ 01 43 54 79 22, Ⓜ Cardinal Lemoine

The Bottle Shop An American-owned restaurant/bar that draws a diverse and faithful clientele, including many international students—and one of the few places in Paris where you can order a pitcher of beer. Ⓐ 5 rue Trousseau 75012, Ⓣ 01 43 14 28 04, Ⓜ Ledru-Rollin

Chez Georges This is Paris incarnate—a beloved, unassuming neighborhood wine bar that attracts young and old alike. Ⓐ 11 rue des Cannettes 75006, Ⓣ 01 43 26 79 15, Ⓜ St-Sulpice

Chez Prune The *bobo* hub of the canal St-Martin that offers a terrific terrace, ideally situated for watching the trendy neighborhood tide of humanity go by. Ⓐ 36 rue Beaurepaire 75010, Ⓣ 01 42 41 30 47, Ⓜ République, Jacques Bonsergent

Maxim's Features food, drink, and dancing in a posh, extravagant interior. It's a legendary place that attracts a fittingly glamorous clientele. Ⓣ 01 42 65 27 94, Ⓦ www.maxims-de-paris.com, Ⓜ Concorde

Pop-In The heart of Paris's indie rock scene. On the weekends you'll have to elbow the hipsters out of the way to get a drink, or a seat, or even a place to stand. Ⓐ 105 rue Amelot 75011, Ⓣ 01 48 05 56 11, Ⓜ St-Sébastien-Froissart

Le Truskel Hipsters gather in this always-packed bar to drink pints and dance to Brit-pop. Ⓐ 12 rue Feydeau 75002, Ⓣ 01 40 26 59 97, Ⓦ www.truskel.com, Ⓜ Bourse

Zéro Zéro Happening, hedonistic, and smaller than a studio apartment. Ⓐ 89 rue Amelot 75011, Ⓣ 01 49 23 51 00, Ⓜ St-Sébastien-Froissart

---

TIPPING IN BARS

If your drinks are brought to the table, a service charge of 15 percent is automatically included in your tab, so there is no need to tip. However, if you're especially happy with the service, you can round up the tab. If you order directly from the bartender, no tip is necessary, but again, you can leave a euro or two to express appreciation.

CLUBS

The most well-known Parisian clubs are good for a night of extravagance, but be prepared to dress and spend accordingly. These clubs tend to feature various DJs and themes depending on the night of the week, which generally don't kick off until after midnight. If the club scene isn't your thing, there are also many smaller, more low-key places where you can get your groove on to electronic, '80s, hip-hop, salsa, or other types of music. You'll usually have to pay a cover charge to get in, which is usually in the €10–€20 range (prices often change depending on the night, who's DJing, and other factors). You can sometimes get in for free if you go before a certain time or if you're female. Here are some popular places to check out.

⊘ **Le Baron** Among one of the chicest, most exclusive of Parisian nightspots, hot on the list of *les people* (celebrities) and their hangers-on. Entry free. Ⓐ 6 avenue Marceau 75008, Ⓣ 01 47 20 04 01, Ⓜ Alma-Marceau

Le Batofar Hosts electro, house, and hip-hop, with the occasional live band sprinkled in—on a boat. Entry ranges from free to €13, but it can climb to €25 for big events. Ⓐ 11 quai François Mauriac, Port de la Gare 75013, Ⓣ 01 56 29 10 00, Ⓦ www.batofar.org, Ⓜ Quai de la Gare

La Favela Chic Provides a taste of São Paulo on the Seine, where you can dine and then dance to the sounds of samba, caipirinha in hand. Weekend cover is €10, which includes one free drink. Ⓐ 18 rue du Faubourg du Temple 75010, Ⓣ 08 26 10 07 90, Ⓦ www.favelachic.com, Ⓜ République

La Flèche d'Or Offers a friendly, relaxed atmosphere and funk, disco, reggae, and many other musical styles in a train-station-turned-club. Entry is free to €6. Ⓐ 102 bis rue de Bagnolet 75020, Ⓣ 01 44 64 01 02, Ⓦ www.flechedor.fr, Ⓜ Alexandre Dumas, Gambetta

Le Gibus Offers electro, disco, or '80s, depending on the night of the week, and is no longer the house of rock it was once famous for being. Entry is €15–€20 with one drink included; ladies often get in for free between midnight and 1 A.M. Ⓐ 18 rue du Faubourg du Temple 75010, Ⓣ 01 47 00 78 88, Ⓜ République

Le Nouveau Casino A highlight of the much-hyped Oberkampf neighborhood, this smaller venue attracts those in the know who come to dance to the sounds of renowned DJs and live acts. Entry is generally €5 to €15. Ⓐ 109 rue Oberkampf 75011, Ⓣ 01 43 57 57 40, Ⓜ Parmentier

OPA Plays eclectic, underground music in an environment that's the antithesis of the touristy, cheesy Bastille nightspots surrounding it. Entry is free. Ⓐ 9 rue Biscornet 75012, Ⓣ 01 46 28 12 90, Ⓦ www.opa-paris.com, Ⓜ Bastille

Queen Club A mythic dance spot for lovers of disco, house, and electronic music. Once a strictly gay club, it now welcomes people of all persuasions. Wednesday is ladies' night. Otherwise, entry is €10–€20, which includes one free drink. Ⓐ 102 avenue des Champs-Élysées 75008, Ⓣ 01 53 89 08 90, Ⓦ www.queen.fr, Ⓜ Georges V

Le Rex Club One of the city's temples of techno, where the prices have stayed reasonable and the sound system is reputed to be the best in Paris. Entry is free to €15. Ⓐ 5 boulevard Bonne Nouvelle 75002, Ⓣ 01 42 36 10 96, Ⓜ Bonne Nouvelle

Le Studio 287 Specializes in over-the-top light shows and unique ambiance. It's the biggest club in Paris, situated on the industrial outskirts of the city. Entry is €20. Ⓐ 33 avenue de la Porte d'Aubervilliers 75018, Ⓣ 01 48 34 00 00, Ⓜ Porte de la Chapelle

---

DRINKING LEGALLY

Anywhere alcohol is served, you'll see a notice with the heading *Protection des Mineurs* (protection of minors)—"minors" defined as those under the age of sixteen, which is the legal drinking age in France. This law is rarely enforced, however, and you'll rarely be asked for ID.

LIVE MUSIC

There are dozens of concerts, sold-out and sparsely attended, pricey and free, going on virtually every night in and around Paris. Ticket prices vary and are often very affordable; contact individual venues for details. For comprehensive concert listings, pick up a copy of *LYLO,* a free booklet available at bars, or check www.fnac.fr.

Le Bataclan Welcomes both well-known and obscure acts. It's a musical institution: It existed in its first incarnation under Napoléon III. Tickets are €10–€40. Ⓐ 50 boulevard Voltaire 75011, Ⓣ 01 43 14 35 35, Ⓦ www.bataclan.fr, Ⓜ St-Ambroise

---

La Cigale Brings world-class underground artists to a space that's officially classed as a historical monument. This late-nineteenth-century hall is among the most beautiful in Paris. Tickets are €20–€60. Ⓐ 120 boulevard Rochechouart 75018, Ⓣ 01 49 25 81 75, Ⓦ www.lacigale.fr, Ⓜ Anvers, Pigalle

---

Le Divan du Monde Offers varied sounds, from gypsy bands to hip-hop artists, as well as an upper-level lounge. Tickets are free to €15. Ⓐ 75 rue des Martyrs 75018, Ⓣ 01 40 05 06 99, Ⓦ www.divandumonde.com, Ⓜ Pigalle

La Guinguette Pirate An intimate club on a boat that features diverse, independent musical acts. Tickets are €8 to €20. Ⓐ 11 quai François Mauriac 75013, Ⓣ 01 43 43 86 46, Ⓦ www.guinguettepirate.com, Ⓜ Quai de la Gare

L'Olympia Features some of the biggest names in music, as well as alternative acts. Everyone from Edith Piaf to Jim Morrison has performed here. Tickets are about €25–€60. Ⓐ 28 boulevard des Capucines 75009, Ⓣ 01 55 27 10 00, Ⓦ www.olympiahall.com, Ⓜ Opéra

Le Point Éphémère Schedules experimental and eclectic musical evenings at the very top of canal St-Martin, in a converted factory-turned-concert space/exhibition hall/bar/restaurant. Tickets are €8–€15. Ⓐ 200 quai de Valmy 75010, Ⓣ 01 40 34 02 58, Ⓦ www.pointephemere.org, Ⓜ Jaurès

GAY/LESBIAN NIGHT LIFE

The trendy 4th *arrondissement* section of the Marais is the most concentrated gay neighborhood (its axes are rues St-Croix-de-la-Bretonnerie and Vielle du Temple). Gay-friendly establishments are by no means limited to this part of the city, as bars and clubs spread west toward Les Halles and east toward the Bastille. For comprehensive gay listings—night life, entertainment, and more—check out www.tetu.com.

B4 Le Café A three-story gay bar/lounge, where you can groove to the DJ's electronic beats in the basement Ⓐ 35 rue Sainte-Croix-de-la-Bretonnerie 75004, Ⓣ 01 40 29 44 40, Ⓜ Rambuteau, Hôtel de Ville

L'Insolite A lower-key gay club refreshingly lacking in attitude. Ⓐ 33 rue des Petits Champs 75002, Ⓣ 01 40 20 98 59, Ⓜ Pyramides

L'Open Café A landmark gay spot that hosts one of the most popular happy hours in the Marais. Ⓐ 17 rue des Archives 75004, Ⓣ 01 42 72 26 18, Ⓜ Hôtel de Ville

Le Pulp A girls' club that's more intimate than your average nightclub, as well as more open, attracting a mixed homo/ hetero crowd on certain nights of the week. Ⓐ 25 boulevard Poissonnière 75002, Ⓣ 01 40 26 01 93, Ⓦ www.pulp-paris.com, Ⓜ Grands Boulevards

Queen Club See "Clubs" for details.

Le Troisième Lieu A lesbian club that offers cheap food and drinks, kitschy décor, and a groovy DJ. Ⓐ 62 rue Quincampoix 75004, Ⓣ 01 48 04 85 64, Ⓦ www.letroisiemelieu.com, Ⓜ Rambuteau

OTHER ACTIVITIES

If you're tired of the bar and club scene, Paris offers plenty of other options to keep you entertained at night, some of which might strike you as incongruous with your surroundings. Whether you want to see how Parisians bowl or how many drinks it takes to make a Frenchman sing, there's no shortage of options—and you'll gain some cultural insight in the process. Try any of these activities.

Bowling Lace up your shoes and line up your pins for an evening of bowling, Paris-style. Students can take advantage of discounts at alleys such as Bowling Mouffetard. Ⓐ 73 rue Mouffetard 75005, Ⓣ 01 43 31 09 35, Ⓜ Place Monge.

Comedy The French have a strong comic tradition (often overshadowed by their intellectual one), and you can even see shows in English at a few places around town. The English-language troupe "Laughing Matters" plays regularly at various venues, and listings can be found on their website, Ⓦ www.anythingmatters.com. For comedy in French, check out the **Café de la Gare.** Ⓐ 41 rue du Temple 75004, Ⓣ 01 42 78 52 51, Ⓜ Rambuteau.

Karaoke If karaoke is your thing, you'll find plenty of places in Paris where you can sing to your heart's content. Just be sure to brush up on your Johnny Hallyday lyrics first. Check out **Restaurant Arizona.** Ⓐ 12 rue de l'Arrivée 75015, Ⓣ 01 45 48 33 34, Ⓜ Montparnasse-Bienvenue

5 COOL DRINKS YOU WON'T FIND AT YOUR COLLEGE BAR BACK HOME

1. **Pastis:** If you like black licorice, try the aniseed-derived apéritif of choice in the South of France.

2. **Absinthe:** See what the hallucinogenic hype is about with a glass of "green fairy," as absinthe is nicknamed. Absinthe has been around for at least two centuries and is produced in part from wormwood—an herb that has been thought to cause insanity. It's illegal in the United States, but perfectly legal in Paris.

3. **Kir:** Craving pre-dinner sweets? Try a *kir,* which is *crème de cassis* (black currant syrup) diluted in white wine. Substitute the white wine with some bubbly to make a *kir royale.*

4. **Desperados:** An ocean away from Mexico, you may be hard-pressed to find good tequila in France. Learn to love France's brand of tequila-flavored beer, Desperados, instead.

5. **Calvados:** For those fond of spirits, try a nip of this apple brandy produced in Normandy.

17. Going Away

One of the best things about Paris is its proximity to the rest of Europe. Just a few hours of travel can take you through many countries. While France is the largest European country (excluding Russia), the ever-expanding high-speed TGV (*train à grande vitesse*) helps shrink it and conveniently links Paris with London, Brussels, Amsterdam, and Luxembourg—with further links in the works.

And with the proliferation of low-cost airlines and numerous youth discounts for train travel, there's no reason not to take advantage of a long weekend here or a week or two off there to discover a new city, region, or country. Reserve your tickets well in advance for trips planned during popular traveling periods—the winter holidays, February and April breaks, and August—to guarantee getting a seat and avoid paying a fortune.

EURAIL

A Eurail pass may be the best option if you want to see many towns, cities, and countries. These popular passes cover trains and ferries and allow deeply discounted travel across eighteen European countries, excluding Great Britain and some countries in Eastern Europe and the Balkans. Eurail passes are intended for visitors and are not generally sold in Europe, so order your pass before you leave the United States or have one sent to you from home. You can place orders directly from the Eurail website (www.eurail.com) or through an online travel service, such as STA Travel (www.statravel.com).

EURAIL OPTIONS

A basic Eurail Pass allows for unlimited travel during a specified period (ranging from fifteen days to three months) and starts at about €400 for travelers aged twenty-five and under. With this pass, you can travel within eighteen European countries, excluding Great Britain and many countries in Eastern Europe and the Balkans. You have several additional options if you can be flexible about your travel dates and destinations. Be aware that the following prices do not include additional costs for high-speed trains, certain ferry lines, and (if you choose comfort over budget) sleeping accommodations on overnight trains. Reservations are mandatory for some high-speed and overnight trains; be sure to book your travel ahead of time during busy vacation periods. You must validate your pass at the train station before boarding the first train, and you must fill in your travel dates on certain passes.

Eurail Global Pass Flexi A good choice if you intend to take sporadic trips, the Eurail Global Pass Flexi allows pass holders to travel on either ten or fifteen days (consecutive or spread apart) within a two-month period. The cost is between about €600 and €800 for youth and €700 and €940 for adults over twenty-five.

Eurail National Pass A Eurail National Pass allows unlimited travel within a specific country's borders for three to ten days (consecutive or spread apart) within a two-month period.

Eurail Selectpass and Eurail Regional Pass A Eurail Selectpass allows you to travel within three, four, or five bordering countries (out of a more extensive list of twenty-two countries) for a specified number of days within two months, while a Eurail Regional Pass allows four to ten days of travel within a two-month period in two neighboring countries. These options can put you out anywhere from €250 to €700 or so, depending on your age and the number of travel days and countries you choose.

THE FRENCH RAIL SYSTEM

SNCF, the French state railroad company, travels through France and beyond and is a remarkably efficient and economical way to get around. You can purchase tickets at any train station, online at www.voyages-sncf.fr, or at any SNCF outlet around town.

If you buy your tickets at least two weeks in advance of your travel date, you can take advantage of SNCF's discounted, nonrefundable *prem* fares (*prem* is an abbreviation of *premier,* which means "first"). Domestic tickets may be purchased or reserved (in which case you have 24 hours to pay) online and picked up later at the station, from train station counters or the automatic machines found at all stations (which generally accept only French bank cards; no cash). International tickets must be purchased at any one of the city's train stations. See "Trains" in Chapter 3 for additional information on traveling by train in France.

THE TGV

The TGV (*train à grande vitesse*) is the French rail system's high-speed train. You'll pay a substantial amount more than you would for a regular train ticket, but the trade-off can be worth it if you're short on time. The sleek, comfortable TGV system connects Paris with dozens of destinations in every direction. In addition to the extensive domestic service available (with the exception of a gaping hole in the center of France), there are numerous international connections (and plans to stretch south into Spain). TGV tickets are purchased like any other tickets through the SNCF. But if you're traveling abroad, you can go directly to the international TGV line's website (www.eurostar.com for the United Kingdom; www.thalys.com for Belgium, Holland, and Germany; www.tgv-lyria for Switzerland).

CARTE 12–25

Pick up a *Carte 12–25* at any French train station. Good for one year, the card gives you 25–50 percent off the ticket price for travel on SNCF trains, including TGV trains, as long as you purchase tickets individually. You'll also get substantial discounts on train travel in other European countries that have an agreement with SNCF. You must be under the age of twenty-six to qualify. For more information, go to www.12-25-sncf.com.

AIR TRAVEL

The discount airline industry is flourishing, and new companies connecting Paris to any number of European cities pop up all the time. Keep in mind that these airlines sell tickets for each leg of a trip separately, so you won't save money by purchasing a round-trip ticket. But this may work to your advantage, as it offers more flexibility in building itineraries. You can easily fly into one city, do some traveling by land, then fly back from another city without having to backtrack.

You can find out which economy airlines fly from Paris to your destination by checking www.flylc.com, a handy site that lets you see every possible city to which you can fly from your chosen departure airport—and which discount airline will get you there. Here are some of the most popular discount airlines that serve Paris.

- **Air Berlin** Ⓦ www.airberlin.de
- **Air Europa** Ⓦ www.aireuropa.com
- **Air One** Ⓦ www.air-one.it
- **Bmibaby** Ⓦ www.bmibaby.com
- **Condor** Ⓦ www10.condor.com
- **EasyJet** Ⓦ www.easyjet.com
- **Germanwings** Ⓦ www.germanwings.com
- **Hapag Lloyd Express** Ⓦ www.hlf.de
- **Myair** Ⓦ www.myair.com
- **Norwegian** Ⓦ www.norwegian.no
- **Ryanair** Ⓦ www.ryanair.com
- **Sky Europe** Ⓦ www.skyeurope.com
- **Thomson Fly** Ⓦ www.thomsonfly.com
- **Vueling** Ⓦ www.vueling.com

UNDERSTANDING DISCOUNT FARES

Before you get excited about great deals like that one-way flight from Paris to Rome you just found online for less than €1, you should know about these catches:

- **Surcharges:** Taxes and fees can tack on an extra €20 or more per advertised fare. Some outfits will even charge you extra for booking by phone. And take note: Baggage restrictions are harsh, so check the requirements online before packing, or you may face steep fees at the airport.

- **Restrictions:** Most sale fares apply exclusively to midweek travel (Tuesday through Thursday) and may involve flying at awkward times. And remember that there are usually a limited number of tickets available at discounted prices. Signing up to receive sale bulletins from airlines can give you an edge in the race for cheap seats.

- **Secondary airports:** Discount carriers often cut costs by using smaller, secondary airports, some of which are less accessible than the major airports. In Paris, you'll have to fly out of the Beauvais Airport.

For travel information to and from Paris's airports, see "To and From the Airports" in Chapter 3.

PACKAGE TRIPS AND TOURS

Throughout the Paris Métro, you'll see advertisements for all-inclusive package trips to sunny vacation spots like Turkey, Tunisia, or Thailand. The prices advertised generally include airfare, hotel, and all meals and drinks, but they don't include tax, travel insurance, and extra activities. You'll also come across ads for package tours, where you'll travel with a guide and a group of other travelers; these may specialize in outdoor adventures like hiking or rafting.

While package trips and tours generally offer great deals, the destination countries tend to be inexpensive, so keep in mind that planning the trip yourself should be equally affordable—and you'll enjoy the freedom of choosing your own day-to-day activities. Here are some popular companies that arrange trips and tours.

Look Voyages A web site with promotions on package deals. ⓣ 08 92 78 87 78, ⓦ www.look.fr

Nouvelles Frontières One of the most well-established French travel companies. ⓣ 08 25 00 07 47, ⓦ www.nouvelles-frontieres.fr

OTU Voyages The best-known French student travel agency. ⓣ 01 40 29 12 22, ⓦ www.otu.fr

Promovacances An Internet tour operator that offers dozens of all-inclusive organized trips. ⓣ 08 99 65 26 50, ⓦ www.promovac.com

http://voyages-sncf.com An SNCF-run website that allows you to search for deals on trains, planes, hotels, and car rentals, and features promotions on package deals to domestic and international destinations. ⓣ 08 92 30 83 08, ⓦ www.voyages-sncf.fr

Wasteels Voyages A student travel company.
℡ 08 25 88 70 70, Ⓦ www.wasteels.fr

A FEW MONEY-SAVING OPTIONS

Here are some discounts that can help you keep your expenses low during your next adventure out of Paris:

AAA Active members of the AAA (Automobile Association of America) in the United States can get discounts on European hotels, restaurants, rental cars, and attractions. Ⓦ www.arceurope.com

Nomads Card The Nomads Card entitles you to discounts at hundreds of hostels throughout Europe as well as reduced rates for Internet access and phone cards. It's available through STA Travel and online. Ⓦ www.nomadsworld.com

VIP Backpackers Card The VIP Backpackers Card will bring you discounts on bus travel, flights, activities, restaurants, and hostels around the globe. It also doubles as a rechargeable phone card. It's available online and through STA Travel. Ⓦ www.vipbackpackers.com

YHA (International Youth Hostel Association) Card You'll need a YHA membership card if you want to stay at one of the thousands of Hostelling International youth hostels around Europe and the world. It also gives you reduced rates at FUAJ (the French branch of Hostelling International) hostels and YHA hostels in England and Wales. Ⓦ www.fuaj.fr

RENTING A CAR

In France, you must be at least twenty-one years old to rent a car. Some companies, however, will add an extra surcharge if you're between the ages of twenty-one and twenty-four, and some companies require a minimum age of twenty-five to rent. Rental cars should run you about €200 a week, not including taxes, gas (more expensive than in the United States), and theft/collision insurance. Some major credit cards provide insurance; contact your credit card company for details. In Europe, rental cars are almost always stick shifts. If you need an automatic, be sure to request it.

CAR RENTAL OPTIONS

The big names in car rentals, Hertz, Budget, Avis, and Europcar, all have branches at the Paris airports, at train stations, and in other locations in Paris. In addition to the major rental agencies, EasyCar (www.easycar.com), the most popular discount online rental, generally offers favorable rates. The catch is that you have to pay up front (nonrefundable) and you're required to return the car to the same place you rented it from. Here are the main car rental agencies serving Paris and France.

- **ADA Dynamic Car** Ⓣ 01 48 06 58 13, Ⓦ www.ada.fr
- **Avis** Ⓣ 08 20 05 05 05, Ⓦ www.avis.fr
- **Budget** Ⓣ 08 25 00 35 64, Ⓦ www.budget.fr
- **Car'Est Location** Ⓣ 01 40 34 58 06, Ⓦ www.cargo.fr
- **Europcar** Ⓣ 08 25 35 83 58, Ⓦ www.europcar.fr
- **Hertz** Ⓣ 01 47 03 49 12, Ⓦ www.hertz.fr
- **Rent-A-Car** Ⓣ 01 42 96 95 95, Ⓦ www.rentacar.fr

You can also book a car rental through these general travel websites, some of which may offer more flexibility in pickup/drop-off locations (and if you use a U.S.-based site, you can pay in dollars rather than euros).

- **Expedia** Ⓦ www.expedia.fr
- **Last Minute** Ⓦ www.fr.lastminute.com
- **Opodo** Ⓦ www.opodo.fr
- **Orbitz** Ⓦ www.orbitz.fr
- **Voyages SCNF** Ⓦ www.voyages-sncf.com

TRAVELING BY BUS

If you're considering traveling by bus, think carefully about what your comfort and time are worth to you. Trains and discount flights are almost always preferable to sitting for hours—or days—on a bus, and they're usually affordable, even for student budgets. That said, Eurolines offers bus service to widespread destinations across the European continent for very competitive prices. The Paris Eurolines terminal is located at the Gallieni Métro station on line 3. Check the Eurolines website for more details.

Eurolines France Ⓣ 08 92 89 90 91,
Ⓦ www.eurolines.com

5 AFFORDABLE IDEAS FOR YOUR SPRING OR MIDTERM BREAK

1. **The Alps:** Many French universities offer cheap package deals granting students a weekend of skiing in the Alps, two to three hours from Paris, for less than €200. You're sure to see these getaways advertised on university bulletin boards. Otherwise, check out student travel agencies such as OTU. ⓦ www.otu.fr.

2. **Organic farms:** If you've got a green thumb, Worldwide Opportunities on Organic Farms (WWOOF) will hook you up with organic cultivators all over France who are willing to take on volunteers for days, weeks, or months at a time. ⓦ www.wwoof.org

3. **Morocco:** The exchange rate between euros and the Moroccan dirham is excellent, and you can try your hand at bartering at Morocco's amazing open-air markets—it's considered impolite if you don't.

4. **Spain:** Take advantage of its proximity and soak up the sun in Spain. Hit Seville to see the awe-inspiring Holy Week processions, which feature thousands of people wearing peaked hoods and carrying candles, or join the crowds in Barcelona, where you can spend your days on the beach and your nights (and early mornings) in trendy dance clubs. You can reach all these destinations by discount airline.

5. **Provence:** Head to this beautiful region in the southeastern part of France. While away an afternoon or two at the markets, cafés, sights, and shops in Aix-en-Provence and Avignon. And don't miss Arles, the real-life inspiration for many of Van Gogh's most famous paintings.

18. Emergencies

t's possible that your time in Paris will be the first time you're on your own, not to mention the first time you're experiencing life in a big city. Although most students can count on the infrastructure of their study-abroad programs to assist in times of need, true emergencies require immediate action.

You should know the number to dial for a medical or legal emergency. Also note the hospital or police department closest to where you live. When all is said and done, the type of emergency you're most likely to face is more along the lines of a stolen MP3 player or wallet. Nevertheless, thinking through potential "what if" scenarios in advance can protect you from experiencing frustration and confusion when you are least prepared to handle them.

> See the "Useful Phrases" section in the Appendix for French phrases to use in the event of an emergency or when talking with the police.

IMPORTANT PHONE NUMBERS

If you find yourself in an emergency situation during your time in Paris, remember one number: 112. This is your all-purpose emergency number, whether you're in need of an ambulance, the police, or you need to report a fire. 112 can be accessed from anywhere in Europe—you'll be connected to local emergency service, just like 911 does in the United States. With its English-speaking operators, this is the best choice for study-abroad students and other travelers. In this section, we'll provide Paris's local emergency numbers. Just remember that if you call one of these numbers, you many not reach an English-speaking operator.

> **112 (Europe-wide emergency services number)** Call this
> number from any cell phone or landline to reach medical,
> police, or fire services; English-speaking operators are
> available. Be prepared with the address of where you are,
> your telephone number, and, if you're calling for someone
> else, the victim's name and age. For more information, go to
> Ⓦ www.sos112.info.

MEDICAL EMERGENCIES

In the event of a medical emergency, rest assured that
French hospitals will receive you and provide excellent
care, regardless of the type of insurance you have. Be
sure to check with your insurance provider to find out
what emergency care and services are covered—well
in advance of an actual emergency. If you're covered
by the French healthcare system, ambulance rides,
treatment, and hospital stays are covered. And if you
do encounter an emergency situation, the following
are the numbers you need to know.

> **15** Call this number from any cell phone or landline for
> life-threatening medical conditions that require immediate
> attention. You'll be put directly in touch with the *Services
> d'Aide Medicale Urgente* (S.A.M.U.), the French national
> medical emergency service, which will dispatch an
> ambulance any time of the day or night.

> **SOS** Médecins/01 47 07 77 77 Call this number if the emer-
> gency is less serious. SOS Médecins is a privately run service
> that provides house call–making teams of doctors twenty-four
> hours a day. English-speaking doctors are available.

FIRE

Not strictly limited to extinguishing fires, French
firefighters are trained and fully able to deal with a
variety of medical emergencies. They have their own
ambulances manned by medical professionals and
work hand-in-hand with the S.A.M.U. and other

organizations to coordinate emergency responses. Fire trucks are generally the first to arrive on the scene, even when ambulances are also summoned, and firefighters carry resuscitation equipment to provide basic life support. A doctor and nurse are often part of the team.

18 Call this number from any cell phone or landline to reach the fire department. Be prepared to provide a precise address or location, including floor number, a telephone number, and the number and condition of any victims. English-speaking operators are available.

CALLING THE EMBASSY

A U.S. consular officer can assist you in the event of a medical or other emergency. Services include helping you locate appropriate medical services, contacting your family or friends, and arranging a money transfer from your bank account in the United States, if necessary.

01 43 12 22 22 Call this number to reach a U.S. consular officer at the U.S. Embassy in Paris, twenty-four hours a day.

POLICE

Every *arrondissement* has one main police station, open twenty-four hours, as well as a handful of branches with more limited hours. In Paris, police are known as the *police nationale,* as opposed to the *gendarmerie,* which generally operate outside of urban areas. For nonemergency situations, find the phone number of your local police station in the *Yellow Pages* (www.pagesjaunes.fr).

17 Call this number to reach the police in the event of an emergency involving crime or violence.

PARIS SAFETY 101

Here are some tips to help keep you safe during your time in Paris:

- **Door codes:** Nearly every apartment building has an entry code that you must type into a keypad to gain access. Many buildings have a second door with an additional *interphone* (code or buzzer).

- **The Métro:** If you're making lengthy transfers alone late at night, stay where you can see other people. There is an emergency button on every Métro platform and an emergency brake inside each train car.

- **Neighborhoods:** Paris is generally very safe, and you can feel comfortable venturing to any neighborhood during the day or even at night if you're with a friend. If you're alone, however, try to stay on streets that are well lit and have other people on them.

- **Pickpockets:** Watch out for pickpockets in Métro stations, touristy areas, and crowded spots such as Les Halles.

GETTING CITED OR ARRESTED

Chances are good that you'll never have a single interaction with a *flic*, or cop, in Paris. Certain not-quite-legal acts are generally condoned in France (walking around with an open container of alcohol, for example), but there is always a possibility that you'll unwittingly find yourself guilty of a *contravention* (minor violation) and get stuck with a substantial fine.

If you're a suspect in a more serious infraction, you may be brought down to the police station and kept for up to twenty-four hours while an initial inquiry takes place, which may be prolonged by an additional twenty-four hours. When the custody period is over, you will either be charged before a judge or released. Meanwhile, during custody, you have the right to:

- Know why you are being held

- Consult a lawyer

- Remain silent or respond to questioning

- Have an interpreter on hand

- Inform a friend or family member of your situation

If you're arrested, the French police will in most cases contact the U.S. Embassy in Paris. You have the right to speak with a U.S. consul, so make sure to exercise that right. The consulate will send a representative anywhere in France within seventy-two hours who will visit you, provide a list of local lawyers if needed, help with financial matters, and contact family and friends. For more information, contact American Citizen Services office at the U.S. Embassy.

Office of American Services Walk-in service hours are 9:00 A.M. to 12:00 P.M. You may call until 6 P.M. daily, and after-hours emergency operators are available.
Ⓐ 2 rue St-Florentin 75001, Ⓣ 01 43 12 22 22, Ⓦ www.franceusembassy.gov, Ⓜ Concorde.

LOST AND STOLEN PROPERTY

Lost-and-found offices are located in all Paris train stations. As quickly as possible, report your lost or stolen item, in person, to the police station that has jurisdiction over the area where the object was lost or stolen. If your loss occurred in the Métro, you can go to any of the city's police stations. At the police station, get a *récépissé de déclaration de perte ou de vol* (official form documenting your declaration), which you may need to replace lost travel documents or make insurance claims. The Paris *Préfecture de Police* has a lost and found headquarters, the *Centre des Objets Trouvés*, where you can go to verify whether your objects have been recovered.

Centre des Objets Trouvés Open 8:00 A.M. to 5:00 P.M. Monday through Thursday and 8:30 A.M. to 4:30 P.M. Friday. Ⓐ 36 rue des Morillons 75015, ⓣ 08 21 00 25 25

REPLACING A PASSPORT

If your passport is stolen, report the theft first to the police and then to the U.S. Embassy. To replace your passport, go in person to the passport office in the embassy's consular section (no appointment is necessary) and bring the items in the checklist. If you have immediate travel plans, you can get an emergency passport, which can often be issued on the same day you apply. It will be valid for a limited time, cannot be extended, and must be exchanged for a regular passport as soon as you return from your trip. If you don't expect to travel for some time, you can apply for a regular replacement passport, which you will receive in approximately two weeks. You can exchange your emergency passport for a regular passport either in France or in the United States.

REPLACEMENT PASSPORT CHECKLIST

Here's what you'll need to bring with you when you apply for a replacement passport:

- ✔ Completed forms DS-11 (Passport Application) and DS-64 (Statement Regarding Lost or Stolen Passport) (the forms can be downloaded at www.travel.state.gov)

- ✔ Two identical passport-size photos (photo machines are available at the consulate for a small fee)

- ✔ Proof of U.S. citizenship, if possible

- ✔ Any form of identification you have, preferably with a photograph

- ✔ Fee payment (currently $97) in cash, money order, or credit card (no checks)

UNEXPECTED TRIPS HOME

Should there be a death in your family or other crisis at home while you're living abroad, airlines can sometimes assist you with securing a last-minute flight to the United States. Each airline has its own policy on how to deal with such situations. Some may offer you a bereavement ticket with a flexible return date—however, this type of ticket is usually very expensive and often requires proof that an immediate family member has died. You can almost always find cheaper last-minute fares yourself simply by searching general travel websites such as www.orbitz.com, www.expedia.com, www.opodo.es, and www.travelocity.com, or by checking with the major carriers.

- American Airlines ⓣ 01 55 17 43 41, Ⓦ www.aa.com/fr
- Continental Airlines ⓣ 01 42 99 09 01, Ⓦ www.continental.com/fr
- Delta Airlines ⓣ 08 11 64 00 05, Ⓦ www.delta.com or www.airfrance.fr (partner airline with Delta)

- **Northwest/KLM Airlines** ⓣ 08 90 71 07 10,
  ⓦ www.klm.com
- **United Airlines** ⓣ 08 10 72 72 72, ⓦ www.united.fr
- **US Airways** ⓣ 08 10 63 22 22, ⓦ www.usairways.com

IMPORTANT PHONE NUMBERS AT A GLANCE

Europe-wide emergency number	112
Fire	18
Medical emergencies	15
Police	17

Appendix

PARIS'S ARRONDISSEMENTS

Here is the contact information for the *Mairies* (town halls) for the twenty *arrondissements* in Paris. You may need this information to find out about neighborhood activities and other happenings for the *arrondissement* in which you live.

1st arrondissement ☏ 01 44 50 75 01, Ⓦ www.mairie1.paris.fr

2nd arrondissement ☏ 01 53 29 75 02, Ⓦ www.mairie2.paris.fr

3rd arrondissement ☏ 01 53 01 75 03, Ⓦ www.mairie3.paris.fr

4th arrondissement ☏ 01 44 54 75 04, Ⓦ www.mairie4.paris.fr

5th arrondissement ☏ 01 56 81 75 05, Ⓦ www.mairie5.paris.fr

6th arrondissement ☏ 01 40 46 75 06, Ⓦ www.mairie6.paris.fr

7th arrondissement ☏ 01 53 58 75 07, Ⓦ www.mairie7.paris.fr

8th arrondissement ☏ 01 44 90 75 08, Ⓦ www.mairie8.paris.fr

9th arrondissement ☏ 01 71 37 75 09, Ⓦ www.mairie9.paris.fr

10th arrondissement ☏ 01 53 72 10 10, Ⓦ www.mairie10.paris.fr

11th arrondissement ☏ 01 53 27 11 11, Ⓦ www.mairie11.paris.fr

12th arrondissement ☏ 01 44 68 12 12, Ⓦ www.mairie12.paris.fr

13th arrondissement ☏ 01 44 08 13 13, Ⓦ www.mairie13.paris.fr

14th arrondissement ☏ 01 53 90 67 14, Ⓦ www.mairie14.paris.fr

15th arrondissement ☏ 01 55 76 75 15, Ⓦ www.mairie15.paris.fr

16th arrondissement ☏ 01 40 72 16 16, Ⓦ www.mairie16.paris.fr

17th arrondissement ☏ 01 44 69 17 17, Ⓦ www.mairie17.paris.fr

18th arrondissement ☏ 01 53 41 18 18, Ⓦ www.mairie18.paris.fr

19th arrondissement ☏ 01 44 52 29 19, Ⓦ www.mairie19.paris.fr

20th arrondissement ☏ 01 43 15 20 20, Ⓦ www.mairie20.paris.fr

USEFUL PHRASES

Here are some of the phrases you'll need to go about your daily life in Paris.

NUMBERS

Phrase	Translation	Pronunciation
0	zéro	*zay-ro*
1	un	*uhn*
2	deux	*duh*
3	trois	*twah*
4	quatre	*kat-r*
5	cinq	*sahnk*
6	six	*seess*
7	sept	*set*
8	huit	*weet*
9	neuf	*nuhf*
10	dix	*deess*
11	onze	*onz*
12	douze	*dooz*
13	treize	*trez*
14	quatorze	*ka-torz*
15	quinze	*kanz*
16	seize	*sez*
17	dix-sept	*deess-set*
18	dix-huit	*dee-zweet*
19	dix-neuf	*deez-nuhf*
20	vingt	*vahnt*
21	vingt et un	*vahn-the uhn*
22	vingt-deux	*vahn-duh*
30	trente	*trahnt*
40	quarante	*ka-rahnt*
50	cinquante	*sang-kahnt*
60	soixante	*swah-sahnt*
70	soixante-dix	*swah-sahnt-deess*
80	quatre-vingts	*kat-ruh-vant*
90	quatre-vingt-dix	*kat-ruh-van-deess*
100	cent	*sahn*
200	deux cents	*duh sahn*
500	cinq cents	*sahnk sahn*
1,000	mille	*meely*

Phrase	Translation	Pronunciation
100,000	cent mille	*sahn meely*
1,000,000	un million	*uhn mee-yon*
first	premier (première)	*pre-myay (pre-MYEHR)*
second	deuxième	*duh-zyem*
third	troisième	*trwah-zyem*
fourth	quatrième	*kat-ree-yem*
fifth	cinquième	*sahnk-yem*
sixth	sixième	*see-zyem*
seventh	septième	*set-yem*
eighth	huitième	*weet-yem*
ninth	neuvième	*nuh-vyem*
tenth	dixième	*dee-zyem*
one-half / a half	un demi / la moitié	*uhn duh-mee / lah mwah-tyay*
one-third / a third	un tiers / un troisième	*uhn tyair / uhn trway-zyem*
one-fourth / a quarter	un quart	*uhn kar*

DAYS OF THE WEEK

Phrase	Translation	Pronunciation
Monday	lundi	*luhn-dee*
Tuesday	mardi	*mar-dee*
Wednesday	mercredi	*mair-kre-dee*
Thursday	jeudi	*zhuh-dee*
Friday	vendredi	*vahn-dre-dee*
Saturday	samedi	*sahm-dee*
Sunday	dimanche	*dee-mahnsh*

MONTHS

Phrase	Translation	Pronunciation
January	janvier	*zhahn-vyay*
February	février	*fay-vree-yay*
March	mars	*marz*
April	avril	*ahv-reel*
May	mai	*mai*
June	juin	*zhwah*
July	juillet	*zhwee-yay*
August	août	*oot*
September	septembre	*sep-tahm-br*
October	octobre	*ok-toh-br*
November	novembre	*no-vahm-br*
December	décembre	*day-sahm-br*

EMERGENCIES & GETTING HELP

Help!
Au secours! / À l'aide!
oh skoor | ah led

Can you help me?
Pourriez-vouz m'aider?
poor-yay voo meh-day

Hurry!
Faites vite!
fet veet

Call an ambulance!
Appelez le SAMU!
ahp-play luh sah-mew

Someone is hurt.
Quelqu'un est blessé.
kel-kuhn ay bless-ay

I need the fire department.
J'ai besoin des pompiers.
zhay bez-wahn day pahm-pyay

I smell smoke.

Je sens de la fumée.

zhuh sahn duh lah fuh-meh

There's a fire in my apartment/apartment building.

Il y a un feu chez moi/dans mon batîment.

il-ee-yah uhn fuh shay mwah/dahn mohn ba-tee-mohn

Call the police!

Appelez la police!

ahp-lay lah po-leece

I need to report a crime.

Je veux déposer une plainte.

zhuh vuh dey-po-say oon plente

I was assaulted.

J'ai été agressé.

zhay-the ah-gress-say

I was mugged.

J'ai été agressé.

zhay-the ah-gress-say

I lost . . .

J'ai perdu . . .

zhay pair-dew

Someone stole . . .

Quelqu'un a volé . . .

kel-kuhn ah vo-lay

. . . my wallet/purse/passport/cell phone

. . . mon portefeuille / sac à main / passeport / téléphone portable

mon por-tuh-foy / sahk ah man / pahs-por / teh-leh-fon por-tahbl

My address is . . .

Mon adresse, c'est le . . .

mon ad-ress, say luh

My telephone number is . . .

Mon numéro de téléphone, c'est le . . .

mon new-meh-ro duh teh-leh-fon say luh

I am on the _____ floor.
Je suis au ... étage.
zhuh swee oh . . .eh-tahj

GREETINGS & INTRODUCTIONS

Hello!
Bonjour!
bon-zhoor

Good morning/afternoon/evening!
Bonjour / bonjour / bonsoir!
bon-zhoor | bon-zhoor | bon-swah

How are you?
Ça va?
sah vah

I'm great/not so great.
Ça va très bien / pas très fort.
sah vah treh byahn | pah treh for

What's up?
Quoi de neuf?
kwah d'nuhf

Nothing much.
Comme d'habitude.
kuhm dah-bee-tewd

What's your name?
Comment t'appelles-tu? / Comment vous appellez-vous?
ko-mah tah-pel-tew | ko-mah voo-zah-play-vo?

My name is . . .
Je m'appelle . . .
zhuh mah-pel

Pleased to meet you.
Enchanté(e).
ahn-shahn-tay

Where are you from?
Tu viens / Vous venez d'où?
tew vee-yehn | voo veh-neh doo

Are you from Paris?
Tu es/Vous êtes de Paris?
tew ay | voo-zet duh pah-ree

I'm from the United States.
Je suis des États-Unis.
zhuh swee deh zet-az-ew-nee

I'm a student at . . .
Je suis étudiant(é) à . . .
zhuh swee zeh-tew-dee-ahn(t) ah . . .

I study . . .
Je fais des études de . . .
zhuh feh deh zeh-tewd duh . . .

Where do you live?
Où habites-tu?/Où habitez-vous?
oo ah-beet tew/oo ah-bee-tay voo

I live . . .
J'habite . . .
zhah-beet . . .

Is this seat/table taken?
Il y a quelqu'un?
il-ee-yah kel-kuhn

How long will you be in Paris?
Tu es/Vous êtes à Paris pour combien de temps?
tew ay/voo zet ah pah-ree poor koh-byehn duh tehm

This is my friend . . .
C'est un ami/une amie . . .
say uh nah-mee/ew nah-mee

Goodbye.
Au revoir.
oh re-vwahr

See you later.
À plus tard.
ah plew tar

GETTING CONNECTED

What's your email?
Quelle est ton / votre adresse mél?
kel ay toh | vote rah-dress mell | ay-mell

What's your phone number?
Quel est ton / votre numéro de téléphone?
kel ay toh | vote new-meh-ro duh teh-leh-fon

I'll call you.
Je t' / vous appelle.
zhuh tah-pel | voo-zah-pel

Call me sometime.
Appelle-moi si tu veux / Appellez-moi si vous voulez.
ah-pel mwah see tew veuh | ah-pel-ay mwah see voo voo-leh

What's your address?
Quelle est ton / votre adresse?
kel ay toh | vote ad-ress

PLEASANTRIES

Please
s'il te / vous plaît
seel teh | voo pleh

Thank you.
Merci.
mair-see

You're welcome.
De rien.
duh ryahn

Excuse me.
Pardon / Excusez-moi / Excuse-moi
par-DON | ex-kew-zay mwah | ex-kewz mwah

Sorry.
Je suis désolé(e).
zhuh swee day-zo-lay

ON CAMPUS

Where/When is your next class?
C'est quand ton prochain cours?
say kahn toh proh-shehn coor

Did you study?
As-tu étudié?
ah-tew eh-tew-dee-yay

Can I look at your notes?
Tu me passes tes notes?
tew muh pass tay not

Want to meet after class?
On se voit après le cours?
ohn suh vwah ah-preh luh coor

I'm going to the library.
Je vais à la bibliothèque.
zhuh vay ah lah bih-blee-oh-tek

Can I borrow your textbook?
Je peux emprunter ton livre?
zhuh puh ahm-pruh-teh toh leev(r)

I forgot my homework.
J'ai oublié mon devoir.
zhay oo-blee-eh moh deh-vwah

I need an extension.
J'ai besoin d'une prolongation.
zhay beh-zwah dune pro-loh-gah-see-yoh

What grade did you get?
Tu as eu quelle note?
tew ah ew kel not

Do you have any idea what's going on?
Tu arrives à suivre?
tew ah-reev ah sweev(r)

I need coffee.
J'ai besoin du café.
zhay beh-zwah de kah-feh

LANGUAGE

Do you speak English?
Tu parles / Vous parlez anglais?
tew parl | voo par-lay ahn-gleh

I speak English.
Je parle anglais.
zhuh parl ahn-gleh

I don't speak French.
Je ne parle pas français.
zhuh ne parl pas frahn-se

I speak only a little French.
Je ne parle qu'un petit peu de français.
zhuh ne parl kuhn p-tee puh duh frahn-se

I don't understand.
Je ne comprend pas.
zhuhn coh-proh pah

Do you understand me?
Vous me comprenez?
voom coh-preh-neh

Speak more slowly, please.
Parlez plus lentement, s'il vous plaît.
par-leh plew lohn-mohn, seel voo pleh

Can you repeat that, please?
Vous pouvez répéter, s'il vous plaît?
voo poo-vay reh-peh-ay seel voo pleh

DIRECTIONS & GETTING AROUND

Where is . . .
Où est . . .
oo eh

What is the address?
Quelle est l'adresse?
kel ay lah-dress

Left
à gauche
ah gohsh

Right
à droite
ah drwaht

Across from
En face de . . .
ohn fass duh

Next to
A côté de . . .
ah koh-tay duh

Behind
Derrière . . .
deh-ree-air

In front of
Devant . . .
duh-vahn

Where's the nearest metro/bus stop?
Où est l'arrêt de bus / Métro le plus proche?
oo eh lah-reh duh bewss | may-tro luh plew prosh

Where can I catch a taxi?
Où est-ce que je peux trouver un taxi?
oo es kuh zhuh puh troo-vay uhn tah-ksee

CONVERSIONS

U.S. TO METRIC

1 in	25.4 mm
1 in	2.54 cm
1 ft	0.3 m
1 sq. ft	0.09 sq. m
1 mile	1.6 km
1 lb	0.45 kg
1 lb	0.07 stone (U.K.)

| 1 oz | 28 g |
| 1 gal | 3.79 L |

METRIC TO U.S.

1 mm	0.039 in
1 cm	0.39 in
1 m	3.28 ft
1 sq. m	10.76 sq. ft
1 km	0.62 mile
1 kg	2.2 lb
1 stone (U.K.)	14 lb
1 g	0.04 oz
1 liter	0.26 gallons

TEMPERATURE

$C = F - 32 / 1.8$
$F = C \times 1.8 + 32$

CLOTHING SIZES

Important note: These sizes are approximate! Always try things on before you buy them. Also note that in the U.K., shoes are not always sold in half sizes, and some stores sell shoes in European or U.S. sizes.

WOMEN'S CLOTHES

U.S.	4	6	8	10	12	14
U.K.	6	8	10	12	14	16
Europe	34	36	38	40	42	44

MEN'S CLOTHES

U.S./U.K.	35	36	37	38	39	40
Europe	46	48	50	52	54	56

WOMEN'S SHOES

U.S.	5	6	7	8	9	10
U.K.	3.5	4.5	5.5	6.5	7.5	8.5
Europe	35	36	37	38	39	40

MEN'S SHOES

U.S.	7	8	9	10	11	12
U.K.	6.5	7.5	8.5	9.5	10.5	11.5
Europe	40	41	42	44	45	47

COUNTRY CODES

Here are some commonly used country codes in Western Europe and North America. Note that many European phone numbers start with a 0, which should only be used when dialing within the country.

Austria	43
Belgium	32
Canada	1
Denmark	45
Finland	358
France	33
Germany	49
Greece	30
Italy	39
Netherlands	31
Norway	47
Poland	48
Portugal	351
Republic of Ireland	353
Spain	34
Sweden	46
Switzerland	41
United Kingdom	44
United States	1

ABOUT THE WRITER

SARA HEFT grew up in Florida and started studying French in high school. Her first sojourn in Paris came at the age of seventeen and apparently left an indelible impression. She decided to go back for a year abroad while studying at Smith College. After graduating in 2003, she promptly returned to her adopted city, where she has since been speaking English for sustenance, studying, freelance writing, figuring out the intricacies of French bureaucracy, and cultivating her garden.

PHOTO CREDITS

1. **Paperwork & Practicalities** © Mick Roessler/Corbis
2. **Neighborhoods** © Richard Walker/Corbis
3. **Getting Around** © PhotoDisc Vol 22/PunchStock
4. **Finding Housing** © Elena Elisseeva/Shutterstock
5. **Shopping** © Carl & Ann Purcell/Corbis
6. **Daily Living** © Seleznev Oleg/Shutterstock
7. **Studying Staying Informed** © ePhoto/Stéphane Chérie/Fotolia
8. **Staying in Touch** © Nigel Silcock/iStockphoto
9. **Health** © Anthony Hall/iStockphoto
10. **Getting Involved** © Carsten Madsen/iStockphoto
11. **Working** © Andreas Guskos/iStockphoto
12. **Fitness & Beauty** © Thomas Lammeyer/iStockphoto
13. **Sports** © Elena Sherengovskaya/Shutterstock
14. **Cultural Activities** © PhotoDisc Vol 22/PunchStock
15. **Eating Out** © K. Thorsen/Shutterstock
16. **Night Life** © Emmanelle Morand/Paulette/Fotolia
17. **Going Away** © Keith Levit/Shutterstock
18. **Emergencies** © DaddyBit/iStockphoto

INDEX